Boardroom Education

T0341717

Michel Syrett and Jean Lammiman

- Fast-track route to designing and delivering educational initiatives aimed at directors and board-level executives

- Covers the key areas of defining the development needs of the Board, designing seminars and programs that inform and inspire their ability to make company strategy, capturing and integrating the contribution of independent directors and managing a wide range of suppliers from business school gurus to boardroom learning specialists

- Examples and lessons from some of the world's most successful businesses including Diageo, Lufthansa, GlaxoSmithKline, British Petroleum Exploration and Lego, and ideas from the smartest thinkers including Jay Lorsch, John Kotter, Charles Hampden Turner, John Adair, Chris Argyris, Richard Dawkins, and Bob Garratt

- Includes a glossary of key concepts and a comprehensive resources guide

TRAINING & DEVELOPMENT

11.04

essential management thinking at your fingertips

First Published 2003 by
Capstone Publishing Limited (a Wiley company)
8 Newtec Place
Magdalen Road
Oxford OX4 1RE
United Kingdom
http://www.capstoneideas.com

CIP catalogue records for this book are available from the British Library and the US Library of Congress

ISBN 1-84112-445-1

Wiley also publishes its books in a variety of electronic formats. Some content that appears in print may not be available in electronic books.

Websites often change their contents and addresses; details of sites listed in this book were accurate at the time of writing, but may change.

Contents

Introduction to ExpressExec

ExpressExec is a completely up-to-date resource of current business practice, accessible in a number of ways – anytime, anyplace, anywhere. ExpressExec combines best practice cases, key ideas, action points, glossaries, further reading, and resources.

Each module contains 10 individual titles that cover all the key aspects of global business practice. Written by leading experts in their field, the knowledge imparted provides executives with the tools and skills to increase their personal and business effectiveness, benefiting both employee and employer.

ExpressExec is available in a number of formats:

» **Print** – 120 titles available through retailers or printed on demand using any combination of the 1200 chapters available.
» **E-Books** – e-books can be individually downloaded from ExpressExec.com or online retailers onto PCs, handheld computers, and e-readers.
» **Online** – http://www.expressexec.wiley.com/ provides fully searchable access to the complete ExpressExec resource via the Internet – a cost-effective online tool to increase business expertise across a whole organization.

» **ExpressExec Performance Support Solution (EEPSS)** – a software solution that integrates ExpressExec content with interactive tools to provide organizations with a complete internal management development solution.

» **ExpressExec Rights and Syndication** – ExpressExec content can be licensed for translation or display within intranets or on Internet sites.

To find out more visit www.ExpressExec.com or contact elound@wiley-capstone.co.uk.

Introduction

An overview of boardroom education.

In 1990, a pioneer of modern boardroom education, Bob Garratt, wrote:

> "Directors are rarely given any induction into their new role or inclusion into their work teams. No time or money is usually made available to them to develop themselves into their direction giving role, so after a few months' struggle, they abdicate the direction giving role and, in their own minds, return to their old specialist job."

What is astonishing about this statement is that, even so recently as a decade ago, it needed to be made at all. The gap in systematic boardroom development was generally unrecognized until the last decade of the twentieth century. Prior to that, boardroom skills were deemed by senior executives to be something one picked up along the way to the top, either as a by-product of one's professional education or experience in the ranks of middle or senior management or by virtue of an old-style high-flyer program.

The price of this neglect is very high. As Garratt pointed out: "The lack of boardroom development means there is not enough energy, time, or diversity of thinking going into the direction-giving policies and strategies of the organization. A vacuum is created where the focus of organizational learning should be."

Yet ironically, it was not was the urgent need for the board's strategic decision making to be overhauled that led to better director development but the lack of transparency and accountability. The poor stock market performance of a significant minority of firms in the wake of the October 1987 crash was accompanied by a series of high-profile clashes between shareholders and the boards of leading US and UK companies, spanning share fixing (Guinness), the travel and entertainment allowances of the chairman (Lone Star Enterprises), and the use of "poison pill" anti-takeover measures (Time Inc. and Paramount).

This led to a turnaround in the attitudes of institutional investors who by then (and still now) owned about three-quarters of the equity of publicly owned corporations. Instead of "doing the Wall Street walk" by disinvesting from corporations whose ethical standards or management performance they had doubts about, they now acted as the owners they theoretically are and used their collective investment clout to overhaul boardroom practices. The role of non-executive chairs and directors as guarantors of the company's integrity and fiduciary probity was taken seriously for the first time in decades.

But it very quickly became evident that raising expectations about the capacity of non-executive directors (NEDs) and non-executive chairs to act as guardians of corporate probity was not enough; nor was an overhaul of boardroom subcommittees governing the appointment, pay, and auditing responsibilities of boardroom directors. To be effective, NEDs needed training and the board needed to act more like an integrated collective. The result was an explosion of seminars, workshops, and individual tutoring sessions offered by specialist institutions like the Corporate Board in the United States and the Institute of Directors in the United Kingdom, as well as business schools focusing on senior management programmes.

This in turn led to a review of the procedures and systematic development of non-profit boards, such as charitable trusts and health or education boards. The focus on the board as an object for continuous development for reasons of probity also led to a welcome review of its role in strategic decision making: an integral part of the "learning organization" therefore became "the learning board."

This ExpressExec title will highlight how these developments have helped to shape the current concepts and techniques used in boardroom education. It will demonstrate that boardroom education is not a tacked-on sub-branch of conventional management development but a distinctive HR function – not least because the individuals on the receiving end have far more influence, and in some cases a veto, on what they are and are not taught.

There are overlaps with the concepts governing management development, individual development, leadership, teamworking, and strategy. Where appropriate, cross-references to the ExpressExec titles focusing exclusively on these topics will be made in the text. However, our strongly held view is that HR practitioners tackling boardroom education need to start from a clean slate. Anyone sponsoring, designing, or delivering a boardroom program will quickly discover that they are in different territory.

What is Boardroom Education?

» Corporate governance-related education
» Strategy-related education
» Individual coaching and tutoring.

As we saw in the Introduction, boardroom education initiatives are prompted by a variety of needs.

» *Corporate governance-related*: inducting and training non-executive directors (NEDs) and chairs; integrating the roles of executive and non-executive directors; developing a team approach by the whole board; compliance with relevant corporate legislation; stakeholder management such as investor, media, and community relations.
» *Strategy-related*: opening up the board to new concepts, developments, and transferable best practice, both from within and outside the organization's own sector; integrating the perspectives and decision-making processes of the board and the senior management team; engaging in brainstorming, think-tanks, and other creative activities concerned with generating ideas.
» *Individual development*: coaching and tutoring in specialist techniques or concepts; board-level performance appraisal (e.g. 360 degree); chief executive or chair mentoring or shadowing.

Let's look at each of these in turn.

CORPORATE GOVERNANCE-RELATED EDUCATION

The principal gap in management development revealed by the renewed focus on corporate governance in the late 1980s (see the Introduction) was that, however talented the executives appointed to the board, the distinction between being a manager and being a director was not made clear to them from the outset.

At the very least, this requires newly appointed directors to understand their legal and fiduciary responsibilities under the law; most importantly that they are personally responsible for any loss or fraud committed by the organization. Yet a 1993 survey by PRO NED, the agency principally responsible for promoting the effective use of independent directors in the United Kingdom, found that while 90% of listed UK companies use systematic means to select directors, only a quarter agree a formal job profile and a letter describing the board's expectations of their role.

Trusting the trust

This applies not only to the directors of publicly owned companies but to a wide range of non-profit, public sector, or charitable posts where the individual is appointed "on trust" to guarantee the financial and ethical property of the organization. One of the beneficial by-products of the crisis in investor relations that led to better director education and development among blue-chip corporations, was that it put a spotlight on the virtual non-existence of proper induction for such posts as school governors, charitable trustees, and the directors of education and health boards.

In the United Kingdom, for example, a 1992 report *On Trust*, published by the Charity Commission and the National Council for Voluntary Organizations, suggested that only half the trustees of national charities had received information about their own role, that of the organization, and about their duties and legal responsibilities as trustees. Only one-third of the trustees of local charities had received the equivalent. Only two-fifths remembered receiving the equivalent. Less than one trustee in ten recalled seeing leaflets outlining the role of trustees from the Charity Commission.

The report recommended a program of courses, induction materials, and briefings that could be readily acquired or taken up by charities. These were developed and launched throughout the 1990s but recent monitoring by the Charity Commission suggests that they have been patchily taken up by charities.

Similarly a 1996 study of non-profit boards in the United States by Barbara Taylor of the Academic Search Consultancy in Washington, DC, and Richard Chait of Harvard University's Graduate School of Education found that the commercial and performance pressures on non-profit organizations are too great for the old governance model to suffice. Under the old model, management defined the problems, assessed options, and proposed solutions. The board merely listened, approved the measures, and monitored.

Under the new model, board and management discover the issues that matter, mutually determine the agenda, and solve problems together. "No chief executive knows enough to be a board's sole supplier of information or counsel." Yet to perform their new role, Taylor, Chait and Holland argue, discussion sessions and briefings are essential to engage and educate the entire board about the issues facing the institution.

Netting the NEDs

Basic education about the legal and fiduciary responsibilities of the board applies to all directors and trustees, whether they hold executive or non-executive positions. Indeed one of the first principles established on basic director induction workshops offered by institutions like the Conference Board in the United States and the Institute of Directors in the United Kingdom is that under the law governing limited liability companies, no legal distinction is made between the two roles. However, the increased focus applied by governments and the institutions on the importance of the role of directors holding non-executive positions to guard and guarantee probity also threw up the dilemma that they would be unable to perform this role unless they benefited from markedly better preparation.

A starting point is proper education for their role as the dominant force on the board subcommittees set up to monitor and determine the appointment of new directors, boardroom pay, and the audit of finances and financial performance. However, NEDs serious about their role quickly find that it is almost impossible to make objective or properly informed decisions about almost any aspect of the organization's affairs unless they are as well informed as their executive counterparts.

This has posed a huge dilemma for those that have championed and pioneered better corporate governance in both the private and public sectors. NEDs are by the very nature of the role part time and once removed from the daily affairs of the organization they monitor. Most either combine their role as NEDs with a full-time executive post in another organization or hold a number of directorships. In terms of both time and energy, it is very hard for any part-time director to acquire the comprehensive knowledge they need to seriously question or challenge the proposals or strategies made by a working executive in full command of the facts and circumstances of his or her case.

The legal requirement for organizations to appoint a majority of NEDs on their boards, or at least on the committees that govern their activities, has been sharpened significantly in many countries over the past decade. The requirement that these directors should be fully briefed and integrated into the day-to-day affairs of the organization is more hazy, simply because there is no clear definition of what level of briefing and integration is sufficient for them to perform the role that governments and the institutions expect of them.

The recent financial collapse of the US conglomerate Enron, entailing a failure of basic principles of corporate governance as scandalous as those of Guinness and Lone Star over a decade and a half ago, highlights how easy it is for ruthless executive directors to circumnavigate the spirit of the law while seeming to sustain its letter.

For those corporations that aspire to uphold the spirit as well as the letter of corporate governance legislation, there are any number of imaginative boardroom education initiatives that will help to achieve this purpose. As we will see in the chapter "State of the Art," companies like GlaxoSmithKline have taken the lead in promoting schemes which enable newly appointed NEDs to establish personal networks and expert knowledge within the organization that will help make proper sense of the paperwork they are legally required to receive before each formal board meeting, and give them the confidence to take the lead in proposing strategies that make the most of the external perspective they bring to the board's affairs.

STRATEGY-RELATED EDUCATION

If the revolution in corporate governance has been one cause of the explosion in boardroom education products and initiatives, then the need to find new ways to inform and formulate strategy has accounted for almost all the rest.

The realization that continuous change is almost the only constant on which organizations can base their assumptions about their future prompted commentators like Gary Hamel and Henry Mintzberg in the early 1990s to argue that strategy as a management discipline was dead (see the chapter "Evolution of Boardroom Education").

Of course, they didn't mean that change alleviated the board or senior management team of the need to make strategy. Quite the opposite. Determining a vision for the future has become the principal *raison d'être* for the leaders of the organization. What Hamel and Mintzberg meant was that the means by which firms plotted their short-term future, based on projections submitted by operational managers and the allocation of resources in a one to five year plan, needed to be replaced by a series of longer term goals or challenges determined by a prediction of what the environment in which the organization operates would be like in a decade or more.

Feeling the way forward

Since no amount of company data or intelligence will in itself enable directors to predict for certain the exactitudes of this vision, gut feeling and instinct have suddenly become respectable. Fred Neubauer and Jagdish Parikh at the International Institute for Management Development in Lausanne have examined how successful executives use instinct to check rational decisions by asking themselves if a decision "feels right."

Neubauer and Parikh found that the synoptic model traditionally used by executives to examine strategic issues – where an individual identifies the problem, clarifies it, generates a series of options, and systematically compares the predicted outcome of each option with the challenges set by the problem – only provides the starting point of the cognitive process that results in the decisions being made.

In a survey of 1300 managers from nine countries, they found Japanese executives using intuition as the final arbiter of choice in just under half the decisions they made and the Americans and British using it two-fifths of the time. "Managers admit using it in a number of areas," says Neubauer:

> "One is 'intuitive discomfort' – when you are in a situation where you 'smell' something is wrong. Even though you can't put your finger on it, you just know there is a problem. Managers use it, too, to check rational decisions by asking themselves if a decision 'feels right'."

Our own work on how creative ideas are inspired and shaped in organizations (see the chapter "Key Concepts and Thinkers"), conducted for the Roffey Park Institute in the United Kingdom, suggests that this gut feeling is not genetically inculcated at birth. Rather it is refined and strengthened by the formative influences of the individuals that make up the decision-making team, including private reading and leisure pursuits as well as knowledge derived from personal or professional networks, and the environment in which creative decision making takes place.

No Mickey Mouse idea

Similarly advocates of diversity such as Disney's Michael Eisner argue that creative decision making stems from a collection of individuals who look at the world differently from each other when examining the same problem from their own unique perspective and applying their individuality to the solution.

All of this has helped to shape the focus and methods used in boardroom education in the last decade. Previously, diversity was achieved by recruitment. Indeed the main incentive for appointing NEDs prior to the corporate governance revolution was to profit from their external perspective (see the case study of Prue Leith in the chapter "State of the Art"). Now chief executives and chairs, sometimes prompted by HR practitioners, see great benefits in exposing board members collectively to new concepts and best practice and letting strategic insights emerge in assessing how they apply to the organization's own circumstances.

The combination of experience and reflection is the central core of any formal initiative. As Europe's principal authority on leadership, John Adair, comments:

"Learning at this level happens when sparks of relevance jump in between experience or practice on the one hand, and principles or theory on the other. One without the other tends to be sterile. It is a common fallacy that strategic leadership is learned only through experience. But experience only teaches the teachable, and it is a school which charges large fees. Strategic leadership is better learned by experience and reflection or thought which, in turn, informs or guides further action.''

Boardroom education initiatives also center around directors' and executives' ability to work as a group. Advocates of team-driven leadership like Meredith Belbin, Andrew Kakabadse, and Jeffrey Sonnenfeld (see ''Key Concepts and Thinkers'') argue that it isn't rules and regulations that hold boards together. It is the way individuals work together. Sonnenfeld, for example, bases the approach used at his Chief Executive Leadership Institute at Yale School of Management in New Haven on how the chair and chief executive work together to create a climate of trust and candor. ''Dissent is not the same as disloyalty,'' he says. ''Leave a board if the CEO expects obedience.''

INDIVIDUAL COACHING AND TUTORING

The lack of any effective preparation for boardroom roles, as opposed to management responsibilities, means that newly appointed directors often require individual tutoring to deal with highly specific gaps in their executive make-up.

In some cases, this may entail confidence building to help executives, used to managing their own baronial fiefs, to cope with peer-based decision making. As we will see in ''State of the Art'', a number of techniques used to coach high-performance sports professionals have been successfully adapted to meet the needs of businesses.

In others, as Bob Garratt explained in the Introduction, a lack of general management education at middle or senior management levels means that the individual lacks the confidence or knowledge to tackle difficult decisions from any but his or her own specialist perspective – a very familiar problem confronting newly appointed directors from an HR background, for example, which often hampers their ability to enter the charmed inner circle of key decision makers (see the chapter ''Evolution of Boardroom Education'').

A third gap, as we have already seen in this chapter, is lack of understanding of the basic legal and fiduciary responsibilities that set directors apart from managers. As outlined in the chapter ''Resources,'' there are any number of courses offered by specialist professional institutes or business schools that can help to bring the individual director or trustee up to speed.

Home alone

Then there are the different and complex needs of the chief executive. As the chief executive of Ambrosetti Great Britain, a specialist consultancy in boardroom education, argued in 1989, those at the very top of an organization, be it government or a business, are almost by definition isolated and feel the need for outside support. "Chief executives are surprisingly lonely. They have no internal friend they can talk to. They can't expose their fears or worries. They cannot show themselves to be what they regard as weak or indecisive."

As we will see in "State of the Art," HR practitioners can have a critical role to play in meeting this need, brokering in and briefing either highly qualified individuals who can act as mentors or sourcing or setting up peer groups that give CEOs from different organizations the opportunity to share experience or best practice. Getting the chemistry right is hard, however, and the chapter looks at the basic dos and don'ts that will help the HR practitioner avoid the pratfalls. The dividing line between personal psychological counseling and business tutoring directly connected to an individual's perspective, management style, and work-based behaviour is, however, very thin. The ethical dilemmas are also discussed in the same chapter.

Chairs as cheer leaders

One beneficial by-product of the corporate governance revolution is that it has enhanced the prestige and distinctive role of the board chair. As we will see in "State of the Art" and "Key Concepts and Thinkers," most effective boardroom education initiatives have resulted from the partnership of an enlightened HR practitioner and a chair with the foresight and authority to gain the support of other, more skeptical directors.

This has been a significant step forward. The characteristic that most distinguishes conventional management development from boardroom education is the participants' right of veto. Unless there are exceptional circumstances, directors cannot be obliged to take part in educational initiatives to which they do not subscribe or feel they do not have time for.

The principle that the chair runs the board, leaving the chief executive to run the company, now extends to ensuring that the board keeps up to date. As Fred Neubauer concludes: "This does not just mean overseeing the hiring or retirement of board members but ensuring that on an individual basis they keep their skills and knowledge fresh and collectively they work as a team."

KEY LEARNING POINTS

» Newly appointed directors, whether executive or non-executive, require a comprehensive induction which enables them to understand and act on their legal and fiduciary responsibilities. This is over and above any training in strategic decision making.

» New concepts of strategy determination, which place a bigger premium on instinct and long-term prediction, require boardroom education initiatives which enable directors (individually and collectively) to test new ways of seeing or doing business against the insight of their own practical experience.

» Personal gaps in knowledge or experience, or in confidence or self-esteem, may require individual tutoring or coaching. This is subject, however, to the strictures laid out in the chapter "State of the Art."

Evolution of Boardroom Education

- » Professional qualifications
- » Military command
- » MBAs and other postgraduate qualifications
- » High-flyer programs
- » The new entrepreneurialism
- » Filling in the cracks.

The best starting point for any look at how boardroom education has evolved is to point out that prior to the 1980s it just didn't happen – at least in any systematic or ongoing way.

Directors were deemed to be qualified for their position by virtue of the experience and education they had picked up along the way. Since this assumption is central to what was wrong with boardroom performance in the mid to late twentieth century, it is worth examining what education and experience newly appointed directors actually picked up along the way – not least because the happenstance nature of this formative pathway is still in place in many organizations today.

PROFESSIONAL QUALIFICATIONS

The first and at one time the only qualification senior managers could offer as evidence of their fitness for the board was the accreditation they received at the end of their original professional education.

This had some substance if the profession was directly central to the activities of the firm – engineering in construction, journalism in publishing, etc. However, some professional institutes went a significant stage further and claimed, either implicitly or explicitly, that this narrowly defined vocational education *in itself* prepared individuals for strategic decision making in senior management or boardroom positions.

Number crunching, boardroom lunching

In the United Kingdom, where the commonest professional qualification held by boardroom directors in the mid twentieth century was accountancy, both the relevant professional institutes and large accountancy practices made highly questionable claims about the extent to which an accountancy qualification prepared newly recruited graduates for a career in general management.

In the absence of any comparably rigorous qualification, there is considerable evidence that an accountancy qualification was already being used in the United Kingdom as training for a general business career before World War I. The ranks of leading business captains in the Edwardian era and the interwar years were dominated by former auditors and bookkeepers. They include Allan MacDiarmid, who qualified as a Scottish chartered accountant in 1905 and, by 1910, had joined the steel makers Stewart & Lloyds, holding the post of secretary and, from 1918, executive secretary and, in 1925, chairman; George Harris, who joined Rowntree as an accountant on qualifying in 1923, and who had risen to be company chairman by 1941; and William Ewing Eadie, who qualified in 1921, Robert Smith (1925), and John Strain (1928), who were all future chairmen of Burmah Oil.

After World War II, the financial function within the largest companies was boosted further, and as a result there was a massive infusion of qualified accountancy staff into all levels of UK management, quadrupling in number from under 20,000 in 1945 to 100,000 in the 1990s. As a result, statements like "training to be a chartered accountant has proved to be an excellent foundation for a career in general management" or "for those who choose not to make their careers with the firm, the training given will fit them for senior positions in other organizations" permeated graduate recruitment literature during the university Milk Rounds of the 1970s and 1980s.

The problem is that while an accountancy qualification was, in fact, an excellent "foundation" for a career in general management, this was only the case if the recipient's perspective was broadened by experience or education in other key business disciplines; and as business became more competitive and bottom-up innovation more essential, financial acumen became no more important than, say, a professional grounding in marketing or HR.

Yet, well into the last decade, UK boards persisted in seeing accurate auditing, balance sheet management, and financial forecasting as virtually synonymous with effective strategy development at director level, while refusing to accord the same pre-eminence to other essential business disciplines.

A major international study carried out by the Cranfield School of Management and Price Waterhouse in 1990 found that while the head of personnel had a place on the board in two-thirds of the 2000 UK firms who responded, only just over half of these were consulted about corporate strategy from the outset and just under a fifth were not consulted at all. Significantly higher proportions of directors with personnel qualifications were intimately involved with corporate strategy among the firms who responded in Sweden and France.

In part, this was caused by the fact that personnel practitioners "stayed inside their professional box" and "failed to talk the language of the board." But in Sweden, where two-thirds of HR directors were closely involved in strategy determination, the survey found that boards were also more inclined to give weight to people issues, while in France, strategy was seen as a truly cross-disciplinary science.

I am what I manage

This contrast is seen in other parts of the world. A survey of 60 multinationals in Hong Kong and Singapore by the Poon Kam Kai Institute of Management found that efforts to introduce total quality management initiatives in the early 1990s were undermined by the insular attitude of senior local managers. Compared to Japan, where a cross-disciplinary approach to management is inculcated from the onset of employment, Chinese managers were much more closeted in their personal psychology. They saw their authority being derived from their professional status rather than their management role. They disliked receiving feedback about their performance as managers and were more reluctant to work with people from different disciplines.

Not surprisingly, when the Hong Kong government overhauled its approach to customer service in the mid 1990s, as part of a public initiative called "Serving the Community," "partnership" was one of the key competencies it sought to inculcate among its managers. Its management strategy stressed: "Change does not occur on its own. It can only happen when people who share the same views and ideas seek each other out and act together. Managers cannot work effectively if they hide behind their specialist functions."

MILITARY COMMAND

Two world wars and a steady stream of minor ones throughout the twentieth century also provided industry with a source of management recruits whose experiences in the field were deemed to qualify them for business leadership in the same unqualified way as accountants' financial prowess.

State defense records from both the United Kingdom and the United States half a century on, for example, suggest that between one-half and two-thirds of all commissioned officers in both countries' armies during World War II wound up in senior management posts. The proportion of former military officers in management is of course significantly less, but the apparent similarities between leading large and very hierarchical military formations into battle and performing a comparable job for a corporation have left a legacy of organization development, leadership, and strategy theory that is still very firmly in place in boardrooms today.

John Adair's concepts of action-centered leadership, still widely practiced in the United Kingdom, were founded partly on his experiences as the only National Service officer in Glubb Pasha's Jordanian Arab Legion and partly on teaching methods he used as a lecturer at the Royal Military Academy at Sandhurst.

Similarly Harvard Business School's John Kotter drew on the US Army's doctrine of military leadership when he developed his approach to change management in the early 1990. "Consider a simple military analogy," he wrote in 1990.

"A peacetime army can usually survive with good administration and management up and down the hierarchy, coupled with good leadership at the very top. A wartime army, however, needs competent leadership at all levels. No one yet has figured how to manage people effectively into battle. They must be led."

As recently as April 2002, *Harvard Business Review* published an article entitled "Maneuver Warfare," which compared how military concepts applied during World War II and the 1991 Gulf War such as "combined arms" operations and "integrated attacks" are mirrored in the commercial strategies of companies such as Capital One and Nutrisystem.

MBAs AND OTHER POSTGRADUATE QUALIFICATIONS

It was precisely to expose executives with narrow professional training or experience to a general and strategic perspective of management that the Master of Business Administration (MBA) qualification was developed in the United States between the wars and exported around the world during the last three decades of the twentieth century.

The MBA's own development from its origins in the 1880s from little more than a course for bookkeepers to a fully blown general management qualification is described in the ExpressExec title *Management Development*. By the early 1960s, the time at which its influence on today's boardroom thinking first became a factor, its structure and content had taken on the form still familiar today. The basic principles are:

» Although a first degree is still a theoretical requirement of most courses, more weight is given to the need for all candidates to have at least three years of practical working experience in a management or quasi-management post prior to joining the program.
» This is because the exchange of views and perspectives between students from different countries, industries, or backgrounds is seen as an integral part of the program.
» To ensure that the program is not diluted by poor intellectual input, all candidates in the best schools around the world are selected using a common examination designed and overseen by the US General Matriculation Admissions Council (GMAC).
» Most programs follow a common structure in which a basic grounding in "core" business functions such as finance, marketing, HR, and operations is followed by the opportunity to apply their principles to the individual's own chosen sector or career path through a series of "elective" courses covering anything from environmental management to strategic communications.

The big houses rule

In theory, these should have resulted in a steady stream of up to 50,000 new managers every year who possess a common set of intellectual skills that will qualify them for the top rungs of management. In practice, this was far from the case. Primarily, the recruitment of MBAs has been dominated by two types of employer – big management houses and investment houses – which together, with the exception of a small dip during the recession of the early 1990s, have snapped up between two-thirds and three-quarters of all candidates from the leading schools. The takers for Columbia Business School's 1996 cadre

Table 3.1

Company	Graduates	Interns	Total
Merrill Lynch	16	21	37
Goldman Sachs & Co.	15	21	36
Lehman Brothers	20	16	36
Booz Allen Hamilton	19	15	34
Citibank	13	13	26
J P Morgan	14	10	24
American Express	10	10	20
Bankers Trust	10	10	20
Coopers & Lybrand	14	6	20
CS First Boston	12	5	17
Morgan Stanley	7	10	17
Bear Steams	6	8	14
Deloitte & Touche	8	5	13
Ernst & Young	10	3	13
Salomon Brothers	7	5	12
Smith Barney	7	5	12
McKinsey & Co	7	3	10
Mitchell Madison Group	8	1	9
Donaldson Lufkin	5	3	8
General Electric	4	4	8
Price Waterhouse	8	–	8
Self-employed entrepreneur	7	1	8
Chase Manhattan Bank	3	4	7
IBM	3	4	7
Union Bank of Switzerland	3	4	7

Source: Columbia Business School, 1996.

(see Table 3.1) is typical of many of the top 20 schools throughout the whole of the 1980s and 1990s.

While between a third and a half of MBAs leave these big firms within five years, it is usually to start their own enterprises or engage in some other form of consultancy or business service provision. This has left the rest of the employment sector feeling ignored and unattractive, a particularly telling criticism being that the emphasis of most MBA programs was too theoretical and analytical. Things came to head during 1990–2 when the top schools experienced a brief downturn in demand from the consultancies and investment houses and looked to industry to make up the shortfall. The resulting thumbs down they received prompted the GMAC to issue a devastating report that culminated in the conclusion that:

> "Dissatisfaction with the conventional MBA splintered. The big university schools, led by Wharton and London, overhauled their curriculum to place more emphasis on cross-disciplinary issues such as quality and globalism in the core course and a greater emphasis on team and project work in the electives. But, welcome though this descent into the real world has been, it has not altered the fact that the dominating influence in the ongoing design of their courses – particularly in providing mid-course internships where students are tested out by potential employers – remain the consultancies and investment houses, that after the brief dip of the 1990s, still recruit the overwhelming majority of graduates."

Big industrial corporations and employers from the public or non-profit sectors have responded differently on either side of the Atlantic. In the United States, large companies with the necessary resources and HR expertise, like Motorola and GE, have established their own corporate universities which offer internal courses geared entirely around the needs of the firm but drawing on external concepts and teaching methods that lend themselves to the industry. In Europe, counterparts have either followed the US model (the NatWest Education and Learning Centre at Heythorpe Park and the Ericsson Management Institute in Stockholm are good examples) or opted for in-company or consortium programs delivered by a leading business school. Either way, the increased focus and practicality of the programs has been achieved at the price of a narrower perspective and a reduced diversity in the background and therefore the contribution of other participants.

HIGH-FLYER PROGRAMS

If professional training and postgraduate management education provide the two most common points of formal preparation for senior managers, the fast-track development schemes that dominated the succession planning policies of large corporations during the stable postwar decades provide the most common career path that linked them together.

Snakes and ladders

Fast-track schemes were born out of the need to circumnavigate the complex ladder of company hierarchies that, in the eyes of the designers, might result in talented individuals being lost to promotion through the happenstance of corporate politics. Tom Glynn Jones, BP's HR manager in the late 1980s, explained the attraction in an interview conducted at the time for the *Sunday Times*:

> "If, as in this country, you recruit your managers after their first degree and you want to get them to the top levels of management in time for them to be of any use, you have at most about 20 years. With the number of management levels they need to go through and the different range of experiences they will require, this is not a very long time."

The keys to these fast-track strategies were:

» early selection, either through a graduate selection scheme linked to assessment centers and psychological testing, or through an internal scheme targeted at 25–30 year olds, using similar techniques;
» planned career progression, organized through a series of attractive projects and assignments, usually lasting about five years;
» planned succession, to ensure that promising high flyers appear regularly on the shortlist of upcoming senior posts; and
» placement on prestigious external management training courses at top business schools or, as an alternative, action learning programs climbing mountains or fording rivers.

If the HR department's card-index system, planned promotion, and luck worked in unison, then the lucky candidate would find himself (and, in this era, it nearly always was a "him") within sight of senior management positions by his mid thirties. At this stage, the second phase of high flying took over and he was groomed for particular senior posts, usually by moving him between functions to broaden his business appreciation. If, at 35, an aspiring senior executive was blocked in his career at the lower levels of management in a dead-end function (like personnel), he could safely assume that he was not a high flyer and that he must have done something wrong.

The appeal of high-flyer schemes was surprisingly deep seated. They helped the board alleviate its anxieties about the next generation of senior executives, by reassuring it that "something was being done." The board profited from the career expectations of a new generation of baby-boomers leaving college. At a time when the structure of organizations was still vertical and silo oriented, these schemes held out the prospect that good people would not get "lost" and never reach the top. And they had a tremendous appeal to both personnel specialists and business school tutors, because they looked active and modern and provided lots of "fun" training activities with a small group of bright participants.

Icarus descending

In the 1990s, the appeal finally declined. Rapid change in the commercial climate made it harder to predict, decades in advance, what the future requirements of senior managers were likely to be. Delayering made it easier to spot talent from a wider range of sources (e.g. "peripheral" functions like research, technology, and data processing) and less likely that it would get lost in the woodwork. The need and desire to push more women through the glass ceiling also meant that the crucial ages of 30–35 which had dominated fast-track schemes had to become subordinate to the candidate's wish to start a family.

Yet the enduring legacy of fast-track schemes is a cadre of senior managers who are now in boardroom positions, who have a homogeneous perspective of the future of the company, and who still nurse elitist views about what kinds of development are valued, and for whom. This is particularly true of professional partnerships where "the halo effect" is deep rooted and where the kind of general management education provided by an MBA or similar course is lacking at associate level.

THE NEW ENTREPRENEURIALISM

If accountancy and military command were deemed without question to qualify an individual for senior management in the past, to the detriment of the board, the mystique of entrepreneurialism is still live and hot today.

Any number of experienced practitioners and commentators have pointed out that the single-minded dogmatism that equips someone to found and establish a new enterprise is often the last personal attribute to sustain it and help it grow.

To cite two of the many surveys on this subject, Marsha Sinetar of the Massachusetts Institute of Technology undertook a series of interviews of senior executives with entrepreneurial track records working for large organizations and found that their leadership style was often marked by an inability to delegate, cronyism, impulsive behaviour, and condescension. Similarly the UK's leading authority on teamworking, Meredith Belbin, argues that entrepreneurial ability founded on the individual's desire to have a free hand to explore new ideas is often accompanied by a complete failure to grant peers and subordinates the same discretion. "Entrepreneurs often act as if they have no weaknesses," he says. "The more macho they become, the more submissive their colleagues and subordinates. The effect can be so powerful that the very culture of the company, and certainly that of the board, shifts to reflect their favoured style of managing."

FILLING IN THE CRACKS

The pathways by which directors reach their positions have therefore been extraordinarily diverse. Some are promoted purely on the basis of their vocational or practical expertise, others by virtue of accountancy, banking, or other related qualification; some through membership of a fast-track scheme that often places looking good above performing well, others by slow and painful progress through a functional specialism that limits their perspective of business issues; and some from the platform of an open MBA program that places theory and analysis over front-line experience, others through an in-company program that sacrifices a broader perspective of business for industry-relevant concepts and practice.

The situation is complicated still further by the practice – discussed in more detail in the chapter "The Global Dimension" – of appointing executives from overseas companies as a means of enriching the international perspective of a large domestic board; by the tensions between family members and professional managers on the boards of privately owned companies (also discussed in "The Global Dimension"); and by the enlarged role of NEDs, both as "guardians" of the interests of investors and company stakeholders (see the chapter "What is Boardroom Education?") and to provide perspectives from other sectors or industries, at a time when innovative thinking is at a premium (see Figs 6.1 and 6.2 in the chapter "State of the Art").

If we add to the mix the issues discussed in the previous chapter, the chair or HR practitioner responsible for the personal education of individual directors and the collective development of the board as a whole is likely to have to deal with a smorgasbord of habits, behaviors, rigidities, and knowledge gaps. They include:

» newly appointed board members who do not understand their roles as directors;
» functional specialists who cannot take a broad enough view of strategy;
» NEDs who do not have the knowledge, time, or company access to contribute effectively to boardroom discussions;
» boards that are emasculated by the "solo" management style of the chief executive;
» boards which, because of the common background or career path of its members (perhaps because of a narrowly designed fast-track scheme or too much reliance on in-company programs), have a view of the future which is either too homogeneous or too rooted in the past;
» boards that focus too heavily on the immediate needs of the company or industry and are therefore out of touch with transferable good

practice and new management concepts that might benefit the organization;

» boards that are out of touch with specific subgroups in the organization, such as the senior management team, functional or profit center heads, key projects, or cross-functional teams, or broader stakeholders including investors, government (local and national), the media, lobby groups, or local communities (both domestic and overseas) where the organization is active;

» boards confined by the fact that the domestic background of its members leaves them ill equipped to develop an effective international strategy (see ''The Global Dimension''); and

» chief executives or individual directors who have personal issues or development needs that they cannot share or resolve with their colleagues or subordinates.

The biggest issue facing any HR specialist in this field is the need to square the dilemma that, at this level, systematic development to fill these gaps can only take place with the consent (not acquiescence) of the individual; and that he or she may be the person least able to recognize they need it.

''Succession to top leadership is necessarily isolating in that it separates senior executives from others, who now report to them, and leaves them without peers,'' wrote London Business School's Manfred Kets de Vries in a thesis entitled *Leaders who self-destruct: the causes and cures* (see ''Resources''):

> ''This is not helped by the fact that whether consciously or unconsciously, employees feel that their leaders are either infallible or paid to know it all. The result is nobody is around, apart from perhaps their spouse, to point out when they need help.''

This is as true of oligarchies like partners in a professional firm, who collectively fail to see the gaps in their performance as a team, as it is of ''solo'' leaders who surround themselves with acolytes. Much of the challenge of boardroom education, explored in more detail in the chapter ''State of the Art'' is how specialists in boardroom learning, who are often in subordinate or supplier roles, work their way around the denial.

KEY LEARNING POINTS

» The specific needs of directors and boards are complicated by the fact that there has been no common pathway to the top of organizations.

» Since the start of the twentieth century (see Table 3.2), finance-oriented professional qualifications in the fields of accountancy, law, and banking have been deemed to equip their holders for strategic decision making, while others, most notable in personnel, have not.

» MBAs, in the latter half of the twentieth century (see Table 3.2), became the most popular gateway from specialist to general management, yet the diversity of approaches adopted during the last two decades has led to a trade-off between industry-relevant concepts and a broader perspective of business.

Table 3.2 Timeline: formative influences on boardroom director.

Timescale	Formative influence	Experts*
Late nineteenth century	*The director as proprietor or investor*: boards made up of entrepreneurs and their financial backers.	
Early twentieth century	*The director as professional*: rise of the professions and the concept of management as a science. Boards made up of accountants, lawyers, engineers, and bankers.	F.W. Taylor, Frank and Lillian Gilbreth

Table 3.2   (*continued*)

Timescale	Formative influence	Experts*
Mid twentieth century	*The director as military commander*: the experience of command in two world wars heavily influences concepts of business leadership, strategy, and people management. Boards made up of former soldiers.	John Adair, John Kotter
1950–80s	*The director as high-flyer*: rise of fast-track development. Boards made up of carefully selected and nurtured talent chosen and assessed by a senior executive elite.	Wendy Hirsh, Lynda Gratton, Cary Cooper, Charles Cox
1960s–present	*The director as management student*: rise of the MBA and postgraduate education. Mass recruitment of graduates by investment and consultancy houses. Concepts of management heavily influenced by strategic analysis and planning.	Peter Williamson, Philip Sadler

(*continued overleaf*)

Table 3.2 (*continued*)

Timescale	Formative influence	Experts*
1970s–present	*The director as entrepreneur*: a re-emergence of entrepreneurialism as a driving force in business fueled by MBA programs and the dot.com revolution. A welcome by-product to mainstream boards is the injection of new concepts of entrepreneurialism and change leadership. An unwanted by-product on start-up and fast-growth boards is excessive solo leadership, cronyism, and lack of investor accountability.	Rosabeth Moss Kanter, Richard Pascale, Charles Handy
1990s–present	*The director as guardian and policeman*: rise of the NED. The corporate governance revolution results in significant new recruitment of independent directors who lack the time and information to monitor executive strategy and probity. Effective induction and boardroom teamwork and development become a priority.	Jay Lorsch, Adrian Cadbury

Table 3.2 (*continued*)

Timescale	Formative influence	Experts*
1990s–present	*The director as continuous learner*: the emergence of innovation and organizational learning as a competitive force leads in turn to a need for directors to think "outside their box" and broaden their knowledge and perspective of good practice and new business concepts.	Gary Hamel, Bob Garratt, Charles Hampden Turner, Manfred Kets de Vries

*See "Key concepts and thinkers" and "Resources."

» Fast-track schemes, where large resources were focused on a small elite, dominated the way senior managers reached the board during the middle of the twentieth century (see Table 3.2). Although rendered redundant by delayering and rapid change, they have left a legacy of elitism and narrowly focused homogeneity in many organizations.
» The challenge of boardroom education is that the individuals or groups that most need systematic development fail to recognize it, but are in positions where they cannot be forced. Working a way around this denial is the first and foremost task.

The E-Dimension

» Dot.con?
» Dot.competence
» Dot.delivery.

Most innovations transform either what we do or how we think. The Internet does both. That is why it is exceptional. By revolutionizing the access and relationship an individual has with potential suppliers, the Net has obliged virtually all organizations to rethink the way they do business.

This chapter will start by looking at the issues currently dominating the debate about e-strategy, particularly following the dot.com crash of 2001, and then focus on two boardroom-level HR issues that spin off from the debate, namely:

» The changing roles of directors in dot.com companies, and those where the Internet has become a central pivot of marketing, delivery, and customer service.

» The way in which technology is changing (or isn't) the way in which boardroom education is delivered.

DOT.CON?

As the individuals most obligated to think on behalf on their organization, directors are clearly in the front line of navel gazing that followed the dramatic crash of the dot.coms in 2000. Strategy is under review as never before. In particular, boards are asking themselves whether the "new economy" was a fiction or whether the excessive overvaluation of dot.com stock, rather than how they were or were not using the Internet to transform the economy, lay at the heart of the crisis.

This question formed the heart of a lecture at the London Business School by Eric Salama, group strategy director of the international marketing services group WPP, in September 2001. Salama distinguishes in strategic terms between those companies that are using technology to change fundamentally what they are offering their customers and those that are merely delivering electronically what they previously delivered through other methods. But he stresses that the key factor here is recognizing how fast and to what extent the expectations of the organization's customers are themselves being changed by their use of Internet and related technologies.

There is, he argues, drawing on theories outlined in a recent book *Blown to bits*, a play-off between "richness" – by which he means the establishment of a highly personalized relationship with the customer, usually involving human contact over the phone or face to face – and "easy access" in any business transaction.

Much of the first wave of dot.com companies exploited the new technology by providing customers easy access. Lastminute and Amazon both did this, playing on the fact that people didn't want to waste time either setting up and attending a face-to-face meeting or even making a phone call to make simple cost-based purchases that they could just as easily make at the click of a mouse button.

But there are transactions where "richness" is still an essential customer requirement and where transactions over the Net will not provide it. The creative twist is in assessing just how much richness is required, in what form, and how this is likely to change over what period of time.

"Let's take financial services as an example," Salama says:

"Ten years ago, most people would insist on seeing a representative from the company if they were buying a mortgage. Now, a growing number of people don't feel the need. They will use the Net to shop around to find the best supplier offering the most advantageous rate. But, nonetheless, most people will want a human being to speak to at the end of a phone before they make the deal and this is likely to remain the case for some time. This is why banks like First Direct whose transactions are based on phone contact are still rated more highly in terms of customer service than banks where transactions are conducted entirely on-line. The information I need could be provided through the computer but it is a comfort factor to speak to someone.

"However if I am a well-heeled professional with a stock portfolio that needs managing, and trust and confidence in the individual is a key factor, this is a different matter entirely. I will want to get a feel for the manager's know how, experience and integrity and this, at least for the moment, requires at least one and maybe regular meetings because the way I assess all this is likely to be as much through tacit signals as what he or she has to say."

DOT.COMPETENCE

The advent of e-commerce does not just affect the way managers think as executives. It also influences the way they act as directors. In 2001, two professors from the business school at the University of Calgary in Western Ontario, Michael Mather and Malcolm Munro, interviewed a panel of non-executive directors of dot.com businesses who also had external roles as directors or internal roles as executives in other companies, as part of a review of Canadian corporate governance legislation commissioned by the government. The purpose was to investigate whether the challenges, assumptions, and personal requirements of dot.com directors were in any way different from those of other companies. They were, in spades.

Firstly, personal investment in the company – merely an option for directors of conventional companies – was "the price of admission" in the case of dot.com firms. Dot.com chief executives, almost by implication, are self-made entrepreneurs and expect fellow directors to share in the risks if they are to gain the benefits. The dynamics of this relationship are heightened because directors on conventional boards are expected to provide a "safe pair of hands" whereas on dot.com boards they encounter, and are expected to emulate, the lateral mindedness of mavericks, free-thinkers, and boat-rockers who shun traditional boardroom values.

Secondly, they are dropped in the deep end regarding the technology. Little or no induction is provided. One director on the Calgary panel felt that as a group he and his fellow directors were like "infants in a new world" and that the whole experience was a way of "going to school and educating ourselves about the new economy." Deprived of any form of new-member orientation, "not even a whisper," they learned the ropes by trial and error.

As Mather, Munro and Sturmer stress, board members with little Web knowledge face a major challenge trying to keep up with the fast-changing environment in which these companies operate.

> "Directors whose own businesses are in a Web arena feel they are able to stay on top of things because they spend their working hours in a Web environment, reading about industry developments and talking to colleagues. The others must invest significant time after work reading industry publications, exchanging information

with colleagues, and attending business seminars or meetings with a dot-com connection.''

The result is that whereas a director on a traditional board is frequently able to add immediate value by drawing on his or her own extensive relevant business experience, a newly appointed dot.com director faces a major learning curve not because the basic principles of business no longer apply, but because the context of the application is foreign and rapidly changing.

In addition, the volatile nature of the industry brings with it ''incredible stresses, psychological pressures, and time demands.'' Aside from ''keeping up,'' dot.com directors must also find the time to meet far more frequently than do other directors. On a traditional board, directors expect to meet quarterly or bimonthly. Dot.com directors find themselves meeting face to face at least once a month, and even more frequently by conference call.

One director in the Calgary study complained about having to deal with numerous telephone calls and ''a constant bombardment of e-mails'' containing weekly updates of corporate developments. In two other cases, directors reported meeting face to face weekly despite plans to meet only monthly: ''It has to be that way because the pace of play in the technology industry is so fast,'' commented one director. Frequent meetings in turn necessitate greater preparation. Another director commented that ''board service is a real job now. You don't just go once a quarter and rubber stamp things. You have to participate. Your help is required to steer the ship.''

The bottom line, however, is that dot.com directors generally face a far heavier demand on their time than directors on traditional boards. Directors must also have substantial personal energy and a commitment to constant learning and updating, all in the absence of reinforcement in the form of a check for services rendered.

PANEL: THE MANY HATS OF THE DOT.COM DIRECTOR

The study of dot.com directors by Canada's University of Western Ontario (see main text) argues that being an effective dot.com director involves playing many roles and wearing many hats. Generally, the authors argue, few directors will wear every hat. But as the fledgling firm comes together, some may find themselves wearing different hats at the same time.

» *Adviser.* Over the early months and years of the venture, advisers may come and go as needs be, but "advising" is a constant role throughout its existence. The challenge of being a good adviser is to generate trust and confidence, to be able to quickly assess key aspects of a situation, and pass along sound judgment in the face of sometimes great uncertainty.

» *Investor.* Investing in a dot.com is an act of faith, a recognition of promise, and a vote of confidence. Many investors are attracted to dot.coms by the possibility of substantial returns in a short time. But those willing to take the risk may also be called upon later to provide additional infusions of capital to keep the venture alive. Like any gambler, the dot.com investor needs to have both the nerve and the good sense to know when to up the stakes or quit.

» *Mentor.* Being a good mentor involves more than simply possessing and passing along some useful facts. The mentor must establish trust and exercise good judgment. Successful mentors have often enjoyed close personal relationships over the years with senior members of the founder's family.

» *Student.* The dot.com world, though in its infancy, is already complex and full of business models different from those found in the traditional business world. To be effective, the director must be a quick learner and commit substantial time to study and understand this new environment.

» *Visionary.* A dot.com director must be able to recognize the essential kernel of value in an idea but have the talent to spin it into new forms or new directions to ensure survival. This takes vision and great tact.

» *Talent scout.* A dot.com director must be much like a professional talent scout, constantly alert to individuals with the skills and abilities required for the dot.com to thrive. Given the personal network and connections of many dot.com directors, this is not a difficult hat to wear.

» *Strategist*. This is one hat which every director is expected to wear and was cited as one of the most interesting and enjoyable aspects of directorship, because strategy is often the focus of the value added by directors, both individually and collectively A well-thought-out strategy is clear evidence of director participation and can most easily be pointed to as the reason for success or failure.

» *Executioner*. The role of shutting down a new enterprise or perhaps removing the CEO is the most uncomfortable hat to wear. Making such a decision in the first instance, and then having to inform those being dismissed, inflicts pain on everyone involved. Mutual friends or relatives outside the board may be offended, or fail to understand or agree with the course of action. Exchanging the hat of mentor for the hat of executioner can be profoundly distasteful. However, argue the authors, failing to do so may in some cases simply postpone the inevitable, resulting in greater pain and damage in the long run.

Source: "Dot-com directors: not for the faint of heart," by P Michael Mather, Malcolm C Munro, and Flora Sturmer. Ivey Business Journal, March 2001

DOT.DELIVERY

Three conclusions emerge from Mather's and Munro's research.

» The different dynamics of decision making in dot.com companies, and the hands-on role NEDs are expected to play, make an independent directorship in these firms a potent learning ground for any executive wanting to learn more about the New Economy.

» The lack of any new-member induction – ''not even a whisper'' – means that any formal preparation for the role needs to be undertaken by the individual, possibly with the help of the parent company's HR function.

» Exposure to the dynamics of decision making in dot.com companies is increasingly valuable because the conditions in which it takes place – volatile, subject to rapid change, and lacking any financial cushion – are those now affecting more established industries and sectors. Many of the NED roles outlined by Mather and Munro for the dot.coms are also directly relevant to the tasks of directors in more established companies.

But if the Internet revolution is actively shaping the content of senior management programs, it is also influencing the delivery. To date, no external provider has developed off-the-shelf software tailored exclusively for boardroom education. However, schools and consultancies on both sides of the Atlantic have the technological capability to work with internal HR experts to design in-company materials for directors that can be delivered over the Net.

In the United Kingdom, Henley Management School has perfected Net-based interactive conferencing technology that it has used to support projects and assignments carried out by senior managers on its Executive MBA program and in-company senior executive programs for organizations such as Standard Chartered Bank and Cable & Wireless. The London Business School has used similar technology to keep members – nearly all board-level managers – in touch with each other on The Innovation Exchange, a forum for companies to share ideas and experiences and which now boasts over 200 members, including Unilever, Mars Confectionery, and Marks & Spencer.

In the United States, the Global Executive MBA launched by Fuqua School of Business at Duke University, North Carolina, mixes two to three week residential sessions in North America, Europe, and Asia with assignments and interchanges conducted over the Net; Fuqua claims that these methods allow any eligible manager anywhere in the world to take part. The Wharton School of Business has broken wholly new ground with its e-learning platform Wharton Direct, which provides current students and alumni with self-paced learning materials including topics relevant to the board.

Then there are the independent software providers. Again, few of them provide tailored packages for boards or even leadership development, which is still seen as something that can only be provided face to face (see the e-dimension chapter of the ExpressExec title

Management Development). Yet the technological foundation for a boardroom education initiative at a distance is there, given an imaginative contribution from an internal HR expert.

SmartForce, formerly CBT Systems, has built a huge installed base of programs in IT and technical training that give it a foothold in many of the world's largest corporations. Similarly, companies like Pensare and Caliber are attempting to link "granularized" content (content segments broken down into components that can be packaged and customized to individual and organizational needs as opposed to traditional courses), live interaction, facilitation, and on-line networking in an effort to enhance the scale, scope, and speed of education and information delivery.

Companies like U-Next and Quisic (formerly University Access) are providing courses for credit and degrees to help companies develop and retain key talent. Companies like Docent, Saba, and Tacit are developing unique learning and knowledge management technology platforms that not only facilitate but also capture learning, and enable them to store, catalog, and disseminate that learning throughout the company. Centra and Click2learn have highly respected technology and service capabilities. And companies like SMGnet and Provant, not to mention a host of traditional providers, are developing content that can help fuel learning and knowledge creation.

CASE STUDY: LEADERSHIP U

The kind of leadership learning initiative that might emerge from an effective partnership of HR expertise and software technology can be found in Leadership U, a senior management program by Click2 (see the chapter "Resources") and the specialist consultancy Development Dimensions International, based in Bridgeport, Connecticut.

This "pick and mix" initiative combines leadership development modules, performance and assessment support, a chatline, discussion forums, and an interactive conference Website. The leadership modules consist of dozens of two-hour, Web-based training courses that cover topics such as performance management, meeting skills, handling conflict, and change management.

However, as DDI's chief executive Peter Weaver comments, the real value of the initiative is that it combines this menu of conventional Web-based courses with guidance that helps users of the site assess both their progress and performance against a personalized "map" that helps them decide what to study next, reinforced with on-line contact with other participants.

"This site is about leadership development and e-learning courses are just a piece of this," Weaver says. "Another piece is getting support when you are in a jam and being able to piece on all the courses into a long term development programme."

KEY LEARNING POINTS

In the review of e-strategy that followed the dot.com crash of 2000, issues are raised that need to be considered by the boards of all organizations. The key issue is whether the organization is using technology to change fundamentally what it is offering to customers or simply to deliver electronically what it previously delivered through other methods.

The volatile, fast-moving atmosphere of dot.com companies means that newly appointed directors will be thrown into the deep end of the pool and may need help (by either the parent or host company) to bring them up to speed.

To date, no software has been developed that is exclusively tailored for virtual boardroom education. However, numerous schools and consultancies have the technological capability to develop a suitable package in partnership with a client's HR experts. A selected list of these is provided in the chapter on "Resources."

The Global Dimension

» Overcoming cultural barriers
» Reconciling different governance.

Most international training and development initiatives resulted from the explosion in world trade that followed the end of the Cold War. Globalism in the 1990s resulted in internationalism permeating throughout the whole organization, with key teams and projects at all levels made up of nationalities from all countries where the firm had a presence.

But this had been preceded in the previous decade by a similar process on the board, at a time when directors were seen as the fount of all strategy. In the summer of 1988, for example, the top retailer Storehouse had just appointed a Frenchman, Michael Julian, as its chief executive. At the same time, Schoichi Saba, Toshiba's chief executive, was sitting on UK chemical giant ICI's board in company with an American and a West German. Nestlé had just appointed an American to join its board of 15 directors, joining two Frenchmen, a German, and a Spaniard. Forbo, a Swiss firm, was pioneering the concept of a "truly" global board. It was composed of directors from all the 10 countries where it had factories. Meetings were conducted in English, French, or German.

The purpose, then and now, was to transform the way in which the board saw its markets. Most international education initiatives at this level date from this period, not least because it became clear very quickly that the desired cross-fertilization of ideas was not going to take place unless some kind of HR intervention occurred.

OVERCOMING CULTURAL BARRIERS

The first major constraint was the difficulty in reconciling different approaches to achieving consensus and support when making key decisions. Research conducted by Cranfield School of Management's Professor Andrew Kakabadse, based on the responses of 5000 managers in 12 countries, suggests that anything between a quarter and a half feel that members of the senior executive team hold fundamentally differing views on the future direction of their company; and that anything between a third and three-quarters feel there are sensitive issues that merit attention but do not receive it.

Asia, the focus of much of the most intense global expansion, is the most interesting region to examine in this respect. While both Chinese and Japanese companies examined in the research have a high level of consensus on a strategy for the organization – which often matches or exceeds their counterparts in most European countries – many are also perceived by respondents to be poor in tackling the hard issues that arise from its adoption.

In Japan, for example, sensitive issues still tend not to be raised because to do so would generate unacceptable levels of discomfort among certain members of the team. In some cases, senior managers knowingly allow the organization to deteriorate rather than openly face up to the problem. Even in this day and age, many firms baulk at the idea of including a foreigner on the board.

Chinese firms, particularly those on the Pacific Rim that are family run, face similar problems because few people are prepared to openly challenge a chairman who is often the majority shareholder or a person of considerable social standing.

David Lie, chairman of the Hong Kong financial services firm Newpower, argues that this often places the chairman in a difficult position.

> "You have to assess people's body language and expressions more closely because they will not speak out. The style is more to wait until the meeting is over and then request private time with the chairman to voice concerns. This results in few issues being discussed in a team atmosphere."

The solution has been for sporadic or sometimes regular meetings of the board to take place in a variety of countries in which the company has a presence, in an atmosphere where pressing day-to-day issues do not interfere with longer term reflection and/or board team bonding.

KEEPING IT IN THE FAMILY

An early pioneer of this was the chemicals conglomerate Henkel KgaE, the inventor of the first self-active detergent "Persil." Until 1985, Henkel was a family-owned company. In that year, it went public and the then chief executive officer, Helmut Sihler, embarked on a strategy of international growth and acquisition.

Within three years the company had built up its existing network of subsidiaries to the point where it had operations in 40 countries and 35,000 employees worldwide, of whom 18,500 were based outside Germany. Despite its public status, the company retained strong links with the Henkel family, who remained the main shareholders. A member of the family was still chairman of the shareholders' committee (the company retained a continental two-tier board system – see below) and this has had a penetrating effect on its corporate culture.

Every two years senior board members from Henkel's subsidiaries all over the world gather for a meeting in the Henkel family home close to the Düsseldorf headquarters, followed by a reception. The meeting is designed and facilitated to ensure that tricky issues that are not being ironed out at a distance are solved in a relaxed atmosphere.

Largely as a result of the individual and collective work undertaken at these "family" gatherings, a new decision-making dynamic has been fostered. Although it is not a requirement, most local CEOs speak German. The exceptions are Spain and the United States. But it is precisely from these countries, as well as France, that the company has drawn its best ideas. To build on these, a series of international task forces have been created which report back to senior executive teams from particular functions on issues directly relevant to their specialisms. The international nature of all of these bodies has over several decades helped to create a genuinely global perspective of both the company's perspective and resources.

Transferring knowledge across borders

The second HR intervention directly connected to global expansion is to ensure that a proper exchange of strategically important information reaches the board from disparate parts of the corporate network, in circumstances where it has no easy day-to-day access. This might include data, insights, and perspectives from senior executives in:

» local offices of the parent company
» subsidiaries in a conglomerate

» partners in a strategic alliance
» suppliers and distributors.

Internal benchmarking exercises by Standard Chartered Bank revealed, for example, that the board based in Europe (where the bank's business was primarily concerned with corporate and project finance) had more to learn about customer service from the senior executives of its Asian branches (where its business was primarily high street) than it did from its principal competitors. It had simply not bothered to ask.

Knowing me, knowing you

Similarly, the branded foods and drinks conglomerate Grand Metropolitan found that internal rivalry between its subsidiaries – which included Burger King, Pillsbury, J&B, Smirnoff, and Haagen Dazs – was constricting the exchange of strategic information to the barest need to know. The matter came to a head in 1994 when the recently appointed chief executive George Bull wanted to coordinate a more systematic drive into the expanding markets of Russia, India, and China – and found that the vitally important information the board needed was not readily available. A telling cultural barrier was the lack of routine contact and close working relationships between the drinks companies in the group, largely centered around the UK-based and culturally oriented subsidiary International Distillers and Vintners (IDV) and the US-based and culturally oriented cluster of food subsidiaries such as Burger King and Pillsbury.

A series of briefings were organized by the group HR department in London to which senior executives from the operating companies – based in locations as far afield as Florida, California, Hong Kong, Singapore, Delhi, Shanghai, and Moscow – were invited. The events were partly intended to provide the group with face-to-face insights from experienced front-line managers in non-competing companies operating in the target countries. But the primary goal, reflected in the time given over to syndicate discussions and think-tank work, was to allow the board to draw on the rich pool of ideas, insights, and perspectives from the managers of its own subsidiaries that had worked in these regions for years and sometimes decades. A more detailed description of one of these briefings, Spearhead China, is published in the ExpressExec title *Management Development*.

The third type of HR intervention in this field, often initiated by the board chair, is to ensure that non-executive directors in a variety of locations are kept sufficiently in contact with the operating front line to gain the perspective they need to add value to the board's work.

In 1990, the new 15-person board of the pharmaceuticals giant SmithKlineBeecham was augmented by two appointments designed to reflect the cultural diversity of the business: Alain Gomez, chairman and chief executive of Thomson, a French electronics and defense equipment manufacturer; and Bridgit Brevel, chairman of the Vorstand (executive committee) of the German Treuhandanstalt (a company set up after unification to privatize East German businesses). SKB's then chairman, Henry Wendt, was a vigorous champion of more effective corporate governance. He asked the new NEDs to study in detail one of the company's four main commercial activities (pharmaceuticals, animal health, consumer brands, and clinical laboratories) so that they could acquire sufficient knowledge of the business to conduct what he described as a "penetrating interrogation of management."

Under Wendt's personal development plan, the NEDs concentrated on one core business for three years, and then moved on to another until they had achieved a detailed overview of the whole business. "We expected them to spend at least two days and maybe more outside board meetings getting to know their assigned sectors," he says. "If they happened to be in a city where we had a presence on business of their own, we encouraged them to make time to call in."

Assigning a culturally diverse team of NEDs to specific sectors gave the SKB board the insight it needed to tackle the company's executive head-on in discussing future strategy. Wendt argued that the importance of their contribution to SKB required their performance to be questioned to an extent rarely undertaken in other companies – and that, just as NEDs appraise the performance of the company's management, so their own commitment should be scrutinized by the chairman: "I appraised their performance as directors, not their views," he says.

"Have they the depth of knowledge to make a valid contribution to strategic discussions and, if not, what can we do to help them acquire this knowledge and develop themselves more formally for the role they are going to play with the company?"

RECONCILING DIFFERENT GOVERNANCE

Far more than at the lower levels of the organization, the impact of globalisation on boardroom education has been shaped by the contrasting corporate governance structures that exist in different parts of the world.

The Anglo-Saxon model, for example, where entrepreneurs build up a thriving business with the aim of either selling it or going public, has focused education and development work on the need to integrate a new breed of NEDs (who are now seen as the representatives or even the guardians of the interests of external investors) into the day-to-day decision processes of the board as a whole.

This contrasts dramatically with the continental European model, where large investors are represented on the board through a two-tier system, and where the dynasty of the founder seeks to retain (over decades and even centuries) a continuing interest or active involvement in the company. Here the development work focuses on how an incoming breed of professional managers can work effectively with representatives of the family who still often have the right to hire and fire; and how the dominant wishes of both can be reconciled with the interests of smaller shareholders who can exert little or no control over the policy or strategy of the firm.

In the rapidly developing economies of Central Europe and Asia Pacific, the issues are even more complex. The board of a multinational whose equity is owned by a mishmash of institutional investors who have distinctly short-term needs often forges alliances with a tapestry of entrepreneurial family-owned enterprises (such as those founded by the overseas Chinese community); state-run or owned firms with a highly political agenda (such as those run by local governments in Eastern Europe or the Chinese mainland); or even central government agencies (still common in certain African and Asian states).

EXAMPLE: BOARDROOM EDUCATION IN FAMILY FIRMS

Work your way through the curriculum of any senior executive program 10 years ago and you would be hard pressed to find a single reference to a family firm as a source of study or interest.

Now, however, it is a growing focus of both research and consultancy support. Three major European schools – INSEAD in Fontainebleau, IESE in Barcelona, and IMD in Lausanne – have academic chairs on family business. All are conducting important research on aspects of family firm management and are distilling the resulting insights into courses, workshops, and consultancy services targeted at the board.

It is easy to forget that in virtually every part of the world that has not adopted the Anglo-Saxon management and investment model, the family firm is the dominant economic force. They make up 80% of the registered companies in Spain and Switzerland and over 95% of those in Sweden and Italy. Add to this the growing international influence of two Asian diaspora that are founded almost entirely on the family enterprise: namely, the overseas Chinese diaspora, largely Cantonese, which stretches eastward from Singapore across Malaysia, Indonesia, Hong Kong, Australia, California, and Canada; and the Indian diaspora, largely Bengali and Punjabi, which stretches westward from Singapore to the Middle East, Africa, and the United Kingdom.

Professor Alden Lank of IMD, co-author of *The Family Business: Its Governance for Sustainability*, notes that on both sides of the Atlantic during the recessions of the 1980s and 1990s, and throughout the economic boom in South East Asia that came crashing to a halt at the end of 1997, family enterprises were the most effective "locomotives" of the economies in which they were located. "They created jobs," he says. "They were among the few enterprises that were successful enough to pay taxes and they displayed the agility and flexibility to maneuver successfully in the troubled waters of their national economies."

IMD was one of the first schools to spot that family boards needed their own distinctive education and development – and that this focuses almost exclusively on getting their governance structures right. According to Alden Lank's co-author Fred Neubauer, a world expert in the field of corporate governance, this means creating the right institutional structures to manage the relationships between the family itself, the board of directors, and the executive management in charge of running the company on a day-to-day basis.

IMD's pioneering program for owners, directors, and managers, "Leading the Family Business," is based on the premise that most of the boards of family firms go through four distinct phases, each requiring its own governance structures.

» *Stage one*: An entrepreneur founds the company. The family is often involved since it may be run from home and the spouse might provide administrative support or personal advice.

» *Stage two*: The business grows. The family is often distanced from the company because it moves into commercial premises. Over a period of decades the founder remains in control, but during that time brings in professional managers to help run it as well as selling shares to outsiders to raise capital. The children of the founder grow up. Some may be involved with the business, others may not. Typically, the founder makes no attempt to groom a successor because, as Professor Lank puts it, "it reminds them of their mortality. Who wants to think of death?"

» *Stage three*: The crisis. The founder approaches a chosen successor too late. By this time the sons or daughters may be unprepared or unwilling to take over. They may lack training; they may even be about to retire.

» *Stage four*: The management of the firm passes to outsiders but the family retains a majority shareholding. The third and fourth generations grow up and this shareholding is spread between anything up to 50 members. Some may sit on the board and a few may work for the business in an executive capacity. But the majority are linked to the business only by their shares. That suits the incumbent management well because it protects them from hostile takeovers. The market for shares is poor and dividends remain low. Shareholders from outside the family (and few within) smoulder in discontent.

With the help of the IMD team, for example, the Family Council of Damart SA, the French textile firm which is run by professionals but owned by a sixth generation of the Desparture family, was able to develop guidelines with its executive managers to govern the selection of junior family members who wanted to join the firm.

"The local manager has the final say," says Joseph Desparture, a director of the holding company. "The family does not want to interfere. One thing we have learned is that anything imposed from the top by people not directly running the firm does not succeed."

KEY LEARNING POINTS

» Cross-national boards bring cross-national approaches to decision making. Boardroom education initiatives need to take into account that the cultural protocol of decision making – for example, whether one shows dissent publicly or privately – will vary across different nationalities and cultures.

» Cross-national corporate structures, particularly those based around self-operating and culturally independent subsidiaries, often inadvertently restrict the flow of knowledge and learning that passes between boards and senior management teams within the group. HR boardroom briefings and discussions that bring together senior directors and executives from all subsidiaries is one way of breaking down the barriers.

» The continental European corporate governance structure, with its emphasis on direct investor representation and ongoing family ownership, brings with it a different set of education and development issues than the Anglo-Saxon model, marked by early and widespread public ownership. A particular focus for boardroom education initiatives has been the setting up and maintaining of proper dialog between family/investor representatives and professional managers.

The State of the Art

Coaching and counselling.

From an HR practitioner's point of view, setting up any form of boardroom education is an act of persuasion – or, at its best, seduction.

A recent report from the Roffey Park Management Institute by the authors explores the reasons why. Based on a survey of 120 CEOs, main board directors, and senior managers in the United Kingdom, it found that directors and senior managers do, in fact, engage in a great deal of personal research and social activity that benefits their mainstream work. However, they need to call the shots in managing this portfolio and they back away from any formal development initiative where they lose ownership of the agenda.

Serendipity rules in directors' eyes. Approximately half the respondents to the survey are members of industrial or professional networks and over a third are members of a dining club (see Fig. 6.1). Informal

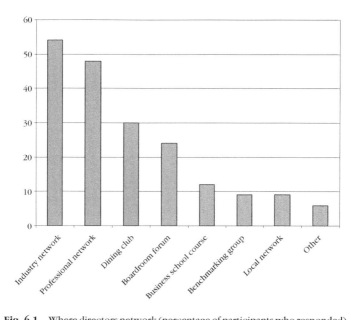

Fig. 6.1 Where directors network (percentage of participants who responded). Source: Roffey Park Management Institute.

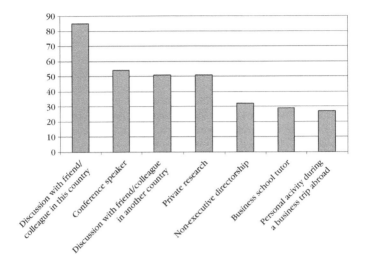

Fig. 6.2   What inspires directors (percentage of participants who responded). Source: Roffey Park Management Institute.

conversations with colleagues and contacts, either in this country or abroad, are highly valued. They form the source for the overwhelming proportion of concepts, ideas, or perspectives that help shape their thinking or inspire specific ideas (see Fig. 6.2).

Privately undertaken learning is also an important source of inspiration. Over half of the respondents get their inspiration from their own private research or hearing a conference speaker and a third from listening to a business school tutor or business academic. It is also interesting that over a third take time out during foreign trips to visit a factory or a local exhibition and that a third cite this kind of activity abroad as a source of inspiration.

Less popular, however, are any events that attempt to capture formally the fruits of this kind of serendipity. Greater numbers of senior managers in the survey opt for informal professional networks or dining clubs than benchmarking groups and boardroom forums where a key activity is to engage in formal syndicate discussion or comparisons of good and bad practice between different organizations.

The key issue here seems to be one of choice. Consultancies or business schools that organize boardroom forums, where attendance is voluntary, often report that one of the most important criteria of whether a senior manager attends an event is careful prior consultation about who else will be there. Senior managers prefer a high degree of control over who they exchange views with. They are more prepared to open up in the informal atmosphere of a professional or industrial network than in formal events where who they consort with and what is discussed is controlled by an external agent.

Trust is the missing factor. "I have a half dozen colleagues in the profession whose views, thoughts, ideas and opinions I value," says Tony Redmond, chief executive and director of finance at the London Borough of Harrow.

> "I meet with them from time to time on very informal terms to talk through these ideas in a way that you would never do even in an action learning set. I am not saying that formal learning sets or courses play no part but you do need exceptional people who you trust to be able to open up and share experiences that really matter."

This does not mean that attempts to set up boardroom learning initiatives are self-defeating. It merely requires a lighter and more responsive approach in the design of the initiative and the way in which in which events are facilitated. Issues include:

» *Prior research*: in any research undertaken to pinpoint key issues and topics to be discussed during the initiative, a cross-section of the participants should be consulted. This will enable the event organizers and the people who are briefing them to check whether their perceptions of the topics and issues to be covered match the agenda of the people who are to be on the receiving end.

» *Recruitment*: the initiative should be run like a club or forum and, as with all clubs, the criteria for membership should be clearly defined and determined by the membership. This is particularly important if participants are made up from more than one organization. If firms are subscribing to a fixed number of places, no substitutes should be accepted.

» *Focus*: while the aim of most boardroom education initiatives is to broaden the perspective of participants and get them to take a balcony view of their work, there needs to be some relationship to the here and now. The starting point to any discussion should be linked to issues that participants are currently grappling or identify with. Otherwise, they will be disinclined either to attend or engage with the process.

» *Flexibility*: the agenda of the program should not be so inflexible as to preclude any shift in emphasis that arises from syndicate or other discussions. Ideally, each session should lead from the previous one. If, for example, a debate about trade with emerging economies unexpectedly reveals a concern among participants about their approach to negotiations, an expert on the subject should be hired in to tackle the issue at the next session. In this way, participants quickly acquire ownership over the topics and begin to see the program supporting their own personal development agenda.

» *Pre-work*: in order to engage participants from the start of each session, a small assignment which they can undertake in a few minutes should be set in the preceding week. This might, for example, be completing a small survey, the findings of which can be fed back to the group during the session. In one session of the executive forum run by the insurance company London & Edinburgh (see the chapter "In Practice"), Professor John Stopford of the London Business School was discussing the importance of collective ambition in revitalizing mature companies. His presentation was based on a large survey of international companies and members of the forum were invited to fill in the questionnaire used for the survey. Professor Stopford was then able to compare the findings of forum members with those of a variety of companies in the survey.

» *Mixed contributions*: Speakers for boardroom sessions should be a mix of leading academics, senior managers from non-competing organizations, and the company's own internal experts. The focus of group discussions should enable participants to examine the issues raised by the external expert's presentation in the context of their own or their company's experiences. This does not have to take the form of conventional syndicate discussion. No standard format for each session needs to be used. Games can make the process of teasing out difficult issues easier for everyone, such as simulations of the BBC's "Question Time" program, where an individual stands up and asks questions arising from the session to a panel consisting of the external speakers and the company's CEO or chair.

» *Sponsorship*: an effective means of ensuring ownership of the content of the program is to cede responsibility for running each session to a member of the group that has a direct interest or expertise in the issue under scrutiny. As "event sponsor," he or she can collaborate with the organizers in choosing and briefing the speaker, and designing any pre-work or syndicate discussion. The event sponsor also chairs the session, setting it in context, introducing the speakers and overseeing the discussions. Wherever possible, the organization's chief executive or chair should "sponsor" the whole initiative. Used in this way, sponsorship is a very effective tool for personal development. It is often a role senior managers are un-familiar with and the consultants organizing the initiative will need to provide them with continuous support and even tuition.

» *Continuous learning between sessions*: learning should not be confined to formal sessions. For a medium-sized company where directors are based on a single site, a newsletter can summarize the learning acquired at each session, reinforcing it for those who attended and allowing those who missed the session to keep in touch with progress. For a larger multi-site or international organization with the right technology, a dedicated Website or discussional database opens up the possibility of group assignments or routine contact between sessions.

Our experience is that the most productive sessions are those where senior managers were able to reappraise current issues in their work from the perspective of a completely different industry or medium. The forum created by London & Edinburgh (see the chapter "In Practice") was at its most lively when its members were encouraged to make comparisons not just between themselves and leading corporates like Rank Xerox and British Airways, which involved conventional benchmarking activities of the type that most members were familiar with, but with organizations like The Kowloon and Canton Railway

Corporation and the Open Air Theatre at Regent's Park, where the points of comparison were more subtle.

In the case of the KCRC, the breakthrough came when forum members and KCRC's chairman realized that the one factor that united an insurance company and a mass transit railway service transporting a million people a day on a 34-mile (55 km) single spur was that customers of both organizations, given ideal circumstances, would prefer not to use the service at all – a realization that led to a highly creative discussion about how customer service should be measured.

Similarly, the Roffey Park survey suggested that many chief executives or main board directors drew heavily on their personal interests in developing an ideal management style. Harrow's Tony Redmond is heavily influenced by his community role as a marriage preparation counselor. David Heslop, chairman of Mazda UK, drew on his love of music when he commissioned a concerto from leading composer Michael Nyman as part of a corporate quality drive. Geoff Morgan, HR director at Lloyd's, finds comedy an extraordinarily effective way of defusing difficult personality issues at work.

The strong impression reached by the research is that these managers, who are at the top of their profession, have not suddenly acquired these interests as a result of their promotion, but reached the point in their careers where they have the freedom and status to admit to and act on the effect of deeply rooted influences. The popularity of the session by Boston Symphony Orchestra's conductor Benjamin Zander at last year's National IPD Conference is an indication of the desire managers at all levels have to dip into their personal interests for work-based inspiration.

If this is the case, there are good reasons why organizations should build managers' personal interests more effectively into their appraisal and development strategies. If a senior manager has a strong interest in sailing, why not give him or her a leading role in designing an outdoor development program which promotes better teamworking or leadership? If comedy is a strong personal interest, why not ask the individual to run a workshop on the right and wrong way to use humor in defusing tension in the workplace or in hosting managers from other cultures? If the individual is a counselor away from work, why not build this skill more effectively into his or her responsibilities at work?

HR interventions of the kind we have discussed here are important because, left to their own devices, senior managers, for all their enthusiasm for networking, still restrict their vision of the world. In the questionnaire-based survey that formed the centerpiece of the Roffey survey, over half of the respondents found inspiration through a conference speaker. Yet follow-up interviews revealed that most senior managers only choose to attend conferences at which they have been asked to speak and since in many cases this related to their own profession or industry, it was not always a mind-opening experience.

Only a third of respondents held non-executive directorships in other companies, admittedly because they often receive scant encouragement from their organization, and those that did usually accepted posts in related industries; and although a high proportion of respondents are school governors or charitable trustees, this often involves them working with people from a similar class or educational background.

HR practitioners often back away from boardroom education because they feel it is more trouble than it is worth. However, if diversity and inclusivity are to be anything more than the latest business fads, the perspective of what are otherwise well-educated managers with expert knowledge of their own industries needs to be extended beyond their own self-imposed borders. Our experience is that the means to achieve this often lie hidden within the managers themselves.

"There is a tendency for managers to be drawn to theories that are driven exclusively by outcomes," says Jenny McIntosh, executive director of the National Theatre.

"I do not look for mechanistic solutions but new ways of thinking that I can feed into the process. This comes from deep within oneself and not necessarily from the stock answers we are exposed to in our day to day work."

NEDs AS AN EDUCATIONAL RESOURCE

Many boardroom education initiatives focus on expanding the perspective or broadening the thinking of busy executives who are too close to the immediate needs of their company to take note of new ideas or interesting good practice.

The immediate instinct of HR practitioners and board chairs is to draw on the expertise of external academics and consultants. An often untapped source of fresh thinking is the board's own NEDs – as the example below illustrates.

Dubbed by the media as "everybody's favorite director," British restaurateur Prue Leith is the living illustration of the benefits of a well-thought-through NED position to the individual and the company.

Leith built her original company, a two-woman catering enterprise, into a £13 million business which she sold in 1993 to the French-owned hotel and travel group Accor. Along the way, there have been two other successful ventures, both sold in 1995. In 1969 she started her restaurant Leiths in Kensington which gained a Michelin star in 1994. In 1975 she founded the School of Food and Wine which she sold to her partner Caroline Waldegrave.

Throughout the 1990s, Leith invested time and energy promoting good practice in industry, focused on her close involvement with the Royal Society of Arts (RSA). As chair of the RSA, she set up an initiative called Tomorrow's Company, sponsored by 25 top corporations, to discover what makes a sustainable, successful enterprise.

The report generated by the initiative was one of the first to introduce the concept of stakeholders and influenced the British Labour Party's economic policies in the run-up to the 1997 General Election which brought them back to power after nearly 18 years in opposition. The project has now been converted into a commercial enterprise promoting what Leith terms an "inclusive" approach to running a business, that is one which engages and consults workers.

Hot off the stove

Leith's interest in good management not only stems from her first-hand experience of running a successful business but from an active role as an NED on the boards of companies outside the catering industry, most notably the brewing giant Whitbread, the supermarket chain Safeway and the Halifax Building Society.

In addition to adding her perspective of the catering industry to key boardroom decisions at the Whitbread Group, most notably in its acquisition and the development of the Café Rouge restaurant chain, she has proved more than just an adornment to the letterhead of the Halifax, largely because of her close working relationship with chief executive Michael Blackburn, who recruited her onto the board of the Leeds Building Society before it was acquired by the Halifax in the early 1990s.

"When I was approached by Michael, I was attracted to the role precisely because I knew little about financial services and I wanted to know more. I told him that I could read a balance sheet but that I had never walked into a branch of a building society or held an account in one. He replied, 'Good, You're a blank sheet. That is what we need.' "

"He wanted someone who could paint a picture of quality and customer service from a different perspective. I in my turn gained a perspective of his industry that has stood me in good stead during my time at the RSA."

Source: "Innovation at the top: where directors get their ideas from," by Jean Lammiman and Michel Syrett, Roffey Park Institute, 1998

COACHING AND COUNSELING

The boost in popularity coaching has enjoyed in recent years (see below) has resulted in a coherent set of procedures which are now followed by most HR practitioners.

James Hunt and Joseph Weintraub of Babson College in Wellesley both run a coaching program that provides a template for the process. This encompasses:

» developing a coaching mindset in the managers who will support the individual (see below);
» assessing whether the individual is "coachable" (see below);
» providing a coaching-friendly context: in particular establishing that the exercise is not about performance appraisal in the context of the company's needs but providing constructive critical feedback that will help the individual assess and resolve issues that are affecting their own work;
» identifying opportunities for coaching arising from day-to-day work;
» maintaining a coaching "mirror": by which they mean keeping an eye on what is important and observing without inferring;
» providing balanced and helpful feedback;
» achieving an agreement between the "coach" and "coachee" on what needs to change in the individual's life and/or work; and
» setting a series of goals arising from this agreement and a program that will enable the partners in the process to review progress.

Whatever process is adopted by the HR practitioner, the success of the exercise will revolve around whether, in Hunt and Weintraub's words, the individual is "coachable."

The essence of most coaching and tutoring is that it covers a range of personal and professional issues that are unique or specific to the individual and that these are discussed in complete confidence and non-judgmentally (see box, "Types of director development").

TYPES OF DIRECTOR DEVELOPMENT
Foundation programs
» legal and fiduciary responsibilities
» essential skills and knowledge (e.g. finance for non-finance directors)
» roles of executives, non-executive directors, and chairs.

Teambuilding
» working across cultures
» achieving consensus

> » getting difficult issues on the table
> » balancing executive and non-executives roles.

Brain opening

> » pushing out boundaries and perspectives
> » informal or formal benchmarking
> » exposure to new ideas and concepts
> » taking directors "outside their box."

Strategy determination

> » leading innovation and change
> » managing investor relations
> » managing diversification and globalization
> » crisis management.

Mentoring/coaching

> » individual leadership
> » managing discussion
> » confidence building
> » filling gaps in knowledge
> » access to a "black box."

However, the most common basis for coaching and tutoring includes any or all of the following:

» lack of knowledge or expertise that makes the individual feel exposed in strategic discussions, but to which they cannot admit publicly;
» inappropriate behavior or management styles (e.g. narcissistic behavior that leads to the individual alienating colleagues or subordinates – see below);
» lack of self-confidence or self-esteem that undermine management performance;
» poor team or project skills that allow the individual to work across boundaries with colleagues on the board or with senior managers; and

» poor "thinking" skills that undermine the ability of the individual to take part in strategic decision making.

These personal issues are closely interconnected and overlap in most coaching or counseling assignments. For example, former McKinsey consultant and Insead graduate Philippa Dickenson set up her own firm The Thinking Partnership which, among other things, coaches individuals in higher level thinking skills. At the heart of her technique, which draws its inspiration from US psychologists' work on incisive thinking, is the assumption that any executive's ability to think through the way to implement key personal and corporate goals is a set of psychological inhibitions and constraints that they can only work through with the support of a "thinking partner" or sounding board. Her work, therefore, not only spans helping executives identify the psychological constraints to clear and incisive thinking but provides them and their colleagues with the non-judgmental listening skills necessary to help work through these constraints – very much in the same way as co-counselors do in psychotherapy sessions.

THE MORE YOU KNOW...

Recent research into what emotional intelligence means in practice by academic thinkers like Daniel Goleman and Danah Zohar suggests that individuals are more self-aware, have a greater tendency to ask "why," and actively seek out uncomfortable situations because they realize that their ability to interpret the environment around them will be enhanced as a result. By contrast, argues team expert Meredith Belbin, "solo" leaders strive for conformity, project their own objectives, and surround themselves with unquestioning acolytes.

Essentially this supports the old adage that the more you know, the more you realize you need to know – and a recent survey by boardroom education specialists The Thinking Partnership and The LSK Group provides additional evidence that this is so.

Thinking Partnership and LSK researchers surveyed 75 chief executives from Top 500 UK companies and found that there was a significant one-third/two-thirds split between those who feel they do devote enough time to strategy and feel well informed about their business (who were in the majority) and those who were less sure.

The interesting aspect of the feedback is that those who raise the most doubts about their performance were better educated, better networked, and come from more modern industries like IT and business services rather than the manufacturing sector.

While only 12% of self-confident respondents state that they draw on the advice and contributions of friends or contacts in their personal networks, in addition to other board members or company consultants over a third of self-doubters did so.

Higher proportions of self-doubters also had postgraduate management degrees (where they would have had the opportunity to step back from their role and examine their business from a broader perspective), argue for greater input from NEDs, and feel that the board should be better informed about front-line practices as well as taking a long-term perspective of the company.

From the perspective of the HR practitioner working with the board chair to better develop individuals in key positions, this suggests that the people most in need of development are often the least able to recognize it.

As Tony Redmond, chairman and commissioner for local government administration in the United Kingdom, who has played a central role in fostering new working practices and standards of working in the public sector, comments:

"I have a half dozen colleagues in my profession whose views, thoughts, ideas and opinions I particularly value. I meet them from time to time on very informal terms to talk through these ideas in a way that you would never do in more formal meetings. I often find that, while I am ahead of them in some areas of good practice, they are ahead of me in others. That thought always keeps me from becoming arrogant."

This presupposes that the person being coached is amenable or capable of responding to the feedback – and it is here that poorly assessed or applied counseling starts to break down. The aim of senior executive coaching is often to make individuals more "emotionally intelligent."

This term was invented by US psychologist and former Wall Street journalist Daniel Goleman who in the mid 1990s looked at the personal profiles of top performers in 500 companies worldwide and found that a high IQ got the best managers only on the first rung of their chosen careers. After that, personal qualities such as an ability to empathize with others and a grasp of the big picture counted for more than analytical skills. At Pepsi-Co, for instance, divisions whose leaders possessed such qualities outperformed others by 15 to 20%.

Goleman's theories stemmed partly from the psychological analysis of business leaders by Harvard Business School's Howard Gardiner, and also a long-term research project undertaken by Harvard University as a whole which examines the neurobiological basis for defensive and non-rational behavior.

The two professors representing the business school, finance expert Michael Jensen, and leading thinker in organizational learning Chris Argyris, are using the results to determine why chief executives persist in making decisions that are bound to damage their companies. They have already concluded that the unconscious mechanisms that generate a fight or flight response in threatened animals generate emotionally defensive behavior in humans.

The all-important process to grasp is this: the signal generating fear in humans reaches the amygdala (the part of the brain at the back of the head which is responsible for our emotions) before it reaches the cortex (the front of the brain responsible for rational thought). As a result, humans are driven into impulsive and defensive behavior by their instincts without being aware of it. If we can learn to temper this instinct, our capacity to make effective decisions is therefore transformed.

Goleman stresses that this newly sought "emotional intelligence" is found in two clusters of personal attributes. The first consist of those qualities the help us become more self-aware: emotional self-control, achievement, and adaptability. The second are those qualities that help us relate better to other people, including the ability to influence, provide effective service, and work well in teams.

"Better self awareness helps people recognize when they are about to be highjacked by their amygdala, and so become better able to short circuit the hijack before they find themselves out of control," he says. "Empathy allows them to do the same for someone else – picking up the early warning signs of irritation, frustration or anxiety that mark a person at risk from a hijack."

But the ability of senior executives to "bypass" their primal instincts is not dependent on training or experience or good-quality feedback. Deeper personality disorders are often involved. Steven Berglas, formerly of the Department of Psychiatry at Harvard Medical School and currently a lecturer at the business school at UCLA, has found that dysfunctional management behavior can often be linked to the narcissistic personalities that prevail at senior management level.

"Narcissists are driven to achieve, yet because they are so grandiose, they often end up negating all the good they accomplish," he says. "Not only do narcissists devalue those they feel are beneath them, but such self-involved individuals also readily disregard rules they are contemptuous of."

The close relationship between individual management failings and personality disorders, especially those linked to personal behavior, is a growing source of worry to Berglas. He points out that executive coaching is a boom industry – at least 10,000 coaches work for businesses today, up from 2000 in 1996 – in which practitioners charge anything between ten and a hundred times more money on a per diem basis than medically qualified psychotherapists.

Yet the majority of executive coaches do not stem from the world of psychology and are an extraordinary mix of former athletes, lawyers, business academics, and management consultants. This is fine when the need of the individual is directly linked to a lack of skills or knowledge that can be rectified by a proven technique, but positively dangerous when it entails a change of behavior or outlook linked to the individual's psychological make-up. No amount of executive coaching, Berglas points out, will alleviate a major personality disorder.

Leadership guru Warren Bennis has also recently aired his concerns. He believes the popularity of executive coaching owes much to the modern craze for easy answers. Business people in general are constantly looking for new ways to change themselves and their companies as quickly and painlessly as possible. A self-help ethic abounds. In this environment of quick fixes, psychotherapy has become marginalized and executive coaches have stepped in to fill the gap. "A lot of executive coaching is really an acceptable form of psychotherapy," he argues. "It's still tough to say 'I'm going to see my therapist.' It's okay to say 'I'm getting counselling from my coach.'"

For the HR practitioner who acts as the "broker" for the individual requiring executive coaching, this necessitates walking a difficult ethical tightrope. The commitment encompassed by the "black box" is that anything the executive wishes to place into it as a personal issue or need to be resolved needs to be responded to in confidence and in a non-judgmental spirit. However, a desire for a socially acceptable quick fix may blind the executive to the deeper psychological causes of the problem.

What seems on the face of it to be an issue of enhancing straightforward strategic decision-making abilities through the application of something that a well-informed management consultant can inculcate, may prove to be a case of hidden clinical depression, well known for blocking an individual's ability to engage in constructive goal-oriented trains of thought. In these circumstances, no amount of conventional coaching will enable the executive to come to grips with the real problems and, in the process, the organization will be incurring wasted costs of anything between £1000 and £10,000 a day at current prices.

Steven Berglas concludes:

"At a minimum, every executive slated to receive coaching should first receive a psychological evaluation. By screening out employees not psychologically prepared or predisposed to benefit from the process, companies avoid putting executives in deeply uncomfortable – even damaging – positions. Equally important, companies should hire independent mental health professionals to review coaching outcomes. This will help to ensure that coaches are not ignoring underlying problems or creating new ones."

See also boxes, 'Issues in director development', 'Benefits of the black box' and 'Assessing and resourcing executive coaching'.

ISSUES IN DIRECTOR DEVELOPMENT

» First catch your director – board members are often suspicious of formal development activity and reluctant to admit their weaknesses.

» Next deal with their pickiness – directors are very choosy about who they rub shoulders with on formal programs; who they are learning with often matters more to them than what they learn.

» Next pick the right tutor – directors are also picky about whose feet they sit at; the tutor has to have a track record of excellence and understand their industries.

» Next design the course right – good director programs take the form of an exchange between peers facilitated by the tutor rather than a classroom lecture.

» Finally sustain their commitment – ensure that their board chair is either a participant or a champion of the program and that the topics under discussion are sufficiently related to "now" issues (e.g. current strategic imperatives) to engage their full participation but approached from a sufficiently broad or lateral direction to broaden their perspective and take them out of their box.

BENEFITS OF THE BLACK BOX

Despite its foreboding title, the "black box" is a beneficial service provided by a number of large employers to staff at all levels, which gives them privileged access to external professionals who act as mentors and guides so that the individual can air and discuss his or her work and career issues. As this service is provided in a black box – that is, it is totally non-judgmental and confidential – it often acts as a diffuser of potentially explosive personal pressures. It is particularly effective at a senior level where the service is kept at a low profile but can be provided at lower levels in the form of well-publicized "employee assistance programs."

ASSESSING AND RESOURCING EXECUTIVE COACHING

» Dissuade senior executives from seeing executive coaching as a "quick fix."
» Screen out executives not psychologically prepared or predisposed to benefit from the process.
» Hire independent mental health professionals to review coaching goals and outcomes.
» Don't assume that executives are the best judge of the benefits or shortcomings of the goals, the outcomes, or the process.

KEY LEARNING POINTS

» The participants of boardroom education initiatives are often self-selecting.
» Influence over what they learn and who they learn with are often key criteria in whether they choose to sign up and engage actively in the process.
» A design which allows the group an ongoing influence over future topics and speakers is therefore best suited to this audience.
» Nonetheless, it needs to be guided and facilitated by either an internal HR expert or an external specialist (or both) who understand how senior executives learn and what bigger issues they need to confront.
» Executive coaching is not always suited to issues of performance, perspective, and behavior that are rooted in personality problems – careful screening should be employed to assess the candidate's and the supplier's suitability to the process.

In Practice

» ITT London & Edinburgh: running a boardroom forum
» BPX: hot groups without the heat
» Royal Ulster Constabulary: supporting change management at the top
» Beachcroft Stanley: educating partners, not directors.

There is an inevitable overlap in looking at examples of good practice between those that highlight effective boardroom education and other concepts such as leadership, senior management teambuilding, strategy determination, and change management.

The case studies in this chapter illustrate the process that under-pins them all. The case on the insurance company ITT London & Edinburgh illustrates the critical triangular relationship that is often required between the board chair who "sells" the initiative to his or her colleagues, the external consultants who bring with them new perspectives and approaches, and the internal HR practitioner who can position these in the context of the organization's current circumstances.

The case on the Royal Ulster Constabulary shows how seemingly esoteric research and consultancy concepts can be grounded in the reality of gritty front-line management circumstances if the chief exec-utive or chair – or in this case the chief constable – has the vision and insight to see the relevance and work hard with the academic or consultant to make the necessary adaptations. The BPX case shows what happens when this does not occur.

ITT LONDON & EDINBURGH: RUNNING A BOARDROOM FORUM

Most of the approaches described in the last chapter were used in a boardroom forum set up by the leading insurance company London & Edinburgh; for example, it was given the express purpose of making the company "Fit for the Year 2005." Made up of the board's strategy group or divisional or business unit heads, it was designed to create a common learning experience between the two groups during a period of intense organizational change.

External presenters were invited to address quarterly meetings of the group, which took place immediately after work in the neutral atmosphere of a local hotel or conference center. These were either leading academic experts or thinkers, or the chief executives or main board directors of organizations in non-competing sectors who had developed good practice in areas in which the group was interested.

Over a three-year period, the group was addressed by directors of organizations such as Rank Xerox on the topic of business process re-engineering, British Airways on sustaining staff loyalty during times of stress, Kent County Council on the effective devolution of budgets and business unit control to front-line managers, and Hong Kong's Kowloon and Canton Railway Corporation on total quality management and customer care. Top academics from the University of Surrey, London Business School, and IMD in Lausanne also made presentations on issues such as business leadership, senior management teamworking, and establishing an innovative and creative culture in the workforce.

Prior reading and the use of "sponsors" for each event drawn from the senior management team, who were chosen for their interest in the topic and who briefed the tutors and the speakers, ensured that the issues raised during the session were sufficiently relevant to the group to "engage" its members in an open debate. The freewheeling discussion that resulted went well beyond the boundaries of the topic in hand, however, turning the forum into a highly creative diagnostic tool in which the company's senior management could test the mood of the heads of their departments and profit centers.

The forum, for example, uncovered the fact that the department heads did not identify at all with the missions and values of the company, as formally stated in the company's literature. As a direct result, a new set of missions and values was developed in collaboration with department heads in which many made highly creative inputs. The forum also highlighted the fact that the innovative potential of the company was being undermined by a "culture of politeness" that made it hard for people to put difficult issues on the table. A working party was set up, headed by the manager who had acted as the sponsor of the event where the issue was raised, to examine ways in which this could be improved.

Finally the forum identified that, while the way in which key business processes were being redesigned was effective and the employment conditions of the staff compared favorably with those of other local companies, more needed to be done to involve and motivate staff at all levels. This was confirmed by a specially commissioned MORI poll which showed that confidence in senior management was not as high as boardroom directors would have liked. Once again, the company is seeking ways to rectify this.

The forum's most significant success was in creating a neutral atmosphere in which members felt free to express their views and follow up lines of thought. No standard format was imposed by the tutors. Syndicate exercises and group work took a different form in each session. The use of unusual organizations – on one occasion, the director of a theater company outlined his own approach to team-working, staff motivation, and customer care and asked members of the forum to help him plan his upcoming season as an exercise – encouraged members to think outside their box and look for analogies and beneficial comparisons in unfamiliar territory.

However, a careful balance was always maintained between focusing on strategic outcomes that benefited the company in the short term, and therefore increased the credibility of the forum in the eyes of the participants and senior managements, and the project's primary task of providing members with a broader perspective of their role and a source of personal development.

The role of "event sponsor," for example, was used to develop key individuals in the group. By giving a different member of the forum in each session the responsibility for liaising with the consultants facilitating the events, briefing the speaker, and "hosting" the session, the organizers ensured that there was a high level of individual and collective ownership over the issues being discussed that reflected the needs and wants of not just the senior executive board members but the departmental heads. Over the years, this also helped build a cadre of committed "product champions" who through their own experience built up an understanding of the real purpose of the project.

It was the view of the organizers that any event of this nature had to be voluntary and there was some concern, borne out by the views in the Roffey Report, that the suspicion of directors of formal development might result in low attendance. In the event, over eight sessions, the attendance was never less than three-quarters of the managers nominated as members.

The role of the chair in championing the project was a significant factor. Taking over the role as chair some weeks after the forum was launched the chairman had been one of the senior boardroom members who had been actively consulted about the format and content and was able to build it into the regular program of boardroom events as one of a number of reforms. In this sense, he was identified closely with its success. He attended all the sessions and encouraged open and at times brutally frank discussions between the strategy group and department heads that would not have been possible in any other environment. He also ensured that feedback from these discussions was followed up, the transformation of the company's mission and value statements being the most important outcome.

The chair is not alone in this role. With the move toward highly defined corporate governance/structures, the role of the chair in not only ensuring that the board's work is transparent, accountable, and ethical but taking responsibility for the board's development has been stressed both by academics and practitioners.

"There has been a longstanding view that if the chief executive is responsible for running the company, the chairman is responsible for running the board," says IMD's Professor Fred Neubauer, director of the school's three-day program for board members.

"However this now extends well beyond making sure that the agenda is kept to. He or she needs to ensure that the board develops in line with the times and reflects the changing nature of the company. This does not just mean overseeing the hiring or retirement of board members but ensuring that on an individual basis they keep their skills and knowledge up to date and collectively they work as a team."

BPX: HOT GROUPS WITHOUT THE HEAT

Bringing together senior managers from different divisions who can explore common business problems has become the fashionable thing to do among cutting-edge companies. However, this will only work if the group has a goal or challenge to focus on. In 1992, an early pioneer of hot groups, the oil and exploration division of BP now known as BPX, established "peer groups" in which leaders of roughly a dozen business units engaged in similar types of businesses met to discuss the strategic and technical challenges they faced. The important thing about these meetings was that board-level management were not allowed in the room.

It didn't work. The exclusion of senior directors may have stopped posturing and encouraged candor but the lack of any strategic purpose reduced the intellectual engagement people brought to the discussions. It was only when the new chief executive of BP, John Browne, based membership of the groups not on whether they were from similar types of business but, regardless of sector, shared similar interests and issues that the groups started to produce results. "You have to have a strong focus on the bottom line to make it worth flying half way around the world for these things," said one member.

ROYAL ULSTER CONSTABULARY: SUPPORTING CHANGE MANAGEMENT AT THE TOP

Few organizations can have confronted such a huge transformation as the one now facing Northern Ireland's nominally civilian police force, the Royal Ulster Constabulary. For the 30 years prior to the Good Friday Agreement that resulted in a terrorist cease-fire in 1998, it functioned more like a paramilitary force than a traditional police service, with 302 officers killed and more than 8000 injured in riots and shooting.

While RUC officers always undertook "ordinary" crime work outside the trouble spots, they have had to become a fully modern operation, with an emphasis on community policing. At the same time, they have had to face continuing outbreaks of politically motivated violence from terrorist groups not on "cease-fire." It is hardly surprising that the top team of the RUC at the turn of the century – the chief constable with his deputy and assistants – considered that some high-impact leadership development was necessary to bring about a change in attitudes. With this in mind, they brought in Cranfield School of Management's Andrew Kakabadse as a consultant, working with the assistant chief constable, Tim Lewis. The aim was to take the RUC's 29 area commanders and turn them into leaders who would be able to change attitudes and behavior in their own areas and be ready to join the top team.

Kakabadse was ideally suited for the task. He has a track record of research and consultancy with UK police authorities, which made it easier for Lewis to "sell" him to top ranks of the RUC who were naturally suspicious of academics with "one black shoe and one brown one." He believes strongly that leadership is a team affair and that the ability of senior managers and directors to forge and exploit common ground is "the" pivotal boardroom skill.

He is also a paid-up member of the "self-development" school of thought that argues leaders are not born, but can be helped to develop themselves. According to Socrates, no one remains "within a box" unless they are constrained by their own perspective. Kakabadse links this to Oriental notions of self-improvement and argues that, despite the impractical nature of the philosophy of enlightenment, these teachings have had a profound impact on management trainers such as Peter Senge and Stephen Covey, who both believe in the ability of individuals to shift perspective and make their own organizations more effective.

Particularly attractive to Lewis was the way Kakabadse himself gives these concepts a necessary injection of street credibility. Kakabadse argues that the behavior demonstrated by senior managers is critical during periods of intense change, if the rest of the organization is to subscribe to the values behind the change. But he also believes that individuals should not be straitjacketed by inflexible "PC" dictats. People in the front line should be given a high degree of discretion in the balance they draw between a management style that upholds the spirit behind the changes and one that will look out of place in the very down-to-earth environment of policing.

His idea of "discretionary leaders" working in teams and able to adapt to the changing circumstances of a volatile environment fitted the RUC's needs perfectly. In the spring of 2001, the area commanders collectively took part in a program of leadership development involving exposure to new ideas, discussion, and self awareness. This culminated in a five-day workshop on transforming community relations.

In the autumn they each spent two days focusing on their own leadership development needs. Part of the process involved keeping a record of the paradoxes they were facing as their roles, and the goals of the RUC, changed. They were also taught the management skills needed to run their own development budgets and take on more management responsibilities as the force moved away from a "wartime" footing.

Lewis was concerned from the start that the real challenge would come when the commanders started to percolate the new ideas and attitudes they had acquired down through the ranks – and he was right. The process has been an uphill struggle for officers still being attacked by youths on the street and still grieving for lost comrades. The controversy sparked over the RUC's change of name has also threatened to derail the process. But the RUC's top team is now united and determined to keep moving on – and, in this, the initiative has been an unqualified success.

BEACHCROFT STANLEY: EDUCATING PARTNERS, NOT DIRECTORS

A survey of 170 partners of UK law firms by the London Business School (LBS) in 1998 found that the legal profession in the United Kingdom is perceived by respondents to be under threat from growing client demands and other professions seeking to enter its jurisdiction.

As a result, firms have reformed or extended their internal managerial controls and taken steps to improve their productivity. About a fifth have merged in the last five years and over a third expect to do so within the next three years. "As with previous mergers, the factors driving the current range of mergers are to strengthen the firm against growing competition and to achieve the right synergies," says Morris. "This suggests that law firms believe they have developed a capability in managing mergers that can be exploited to realise their own unique internal strengths."

Morris also found that between 1995 and 1998, law firms had carried out a number of internal reforms that enable them to compete more effectively. These included, in order of stated priority, introducing quality control policies, measures designed to help partners and administrative staff focus more effectively on client needs, tighter financial controls, and more professional marketing.

Yet moves by the firms to compete in the real world have taken place in the context of an internal culture which smacks of another era. Partner consensus and participation in all decisions are still seen as desirable. Improving the effectiveness of their business development while retaining their professional culture is seen as the main challenge by many senior partners.

Partnership forms of governance also act as a barrier to firms in the LBS survey wishing to introduce reforms. One senior partner comments:

"As a firm we are stuck with a rather old fashioned partnership agreement based completely on lockstep with no performance remuneration. The partnership agreement does not provide for retirement etc from the partnership to retirement age at all. The partnership agreement can only be varied with the consent of ALL partners – and such consent is not forthcoming. The alternative of dissolution ... frightens many of the partners who want a change! A classic example of not being able to deal with underperforming partners! With a tougher and more difficult marketplace today underperformance stands out and causes friction! I am sure and in fact know that we are not alone with this unsatisfactory problem."

The initiatives most associate with reform – quality initiatives, better marketing, tighter financial control – all need to be closely intertwined with management development to prove effective. Beachcroft Stanley, a well-respected medium-sized legal firm employing 300 staff, provides an illustration of good practice in how to assess and meet the training needs of a professional practice in the in-company program it devised for its partners between 1996 and 1998.

The task was given to a newly recruited training manager, Dorita Sheriff, who had previously worked for accountancy firm Arthur Andersen. "Prior to 1996, the firm had provided good technical training and support for professional staff sitting for the Law Society exams," she says. "All other training support was ad hoc and there was no doubt in the minds of the partners that something more systematic was required to provide them with key management skills."

Given that any development program for senior partners would need to be voluntary, the key to its success in Sheriff's view was a sophisticated exercise to analyze their training needs, based on a self-assessment questionnaire. In this way, the topics covered by the program would be those most likely to provoke a high response, therefore validating the initiative in the eyes of any skeptics.

At the same time, Sheriff had to be sure that the partners did not overlook any business skills that would enable them to compete more effectively in an increasingly savage marketplace. "They identified the skills most associated with effective day-to-day management – leadership, teamworking, setting objectives – but they did not come up with any business development skills," she says. "I added on a series of sessions on topics that would not have occurred to them like personal selling skills, developing marketing strategies, event management and persuasive presentations."

Using independent tutors that she had worked with at Arthur Andersen, she designed programs with practical exercises that taxed Beachcroft Stanley's partners in ways never envisaged in their professional education. The session on event management was a good example.

> "You are in a room full of your most respected clients and you have your business cards – so what do you do then? Well to start with, treat it like you would if it was your house. Find out where the toilets are, be courteous and make them feel comfortable."

During the course of a simulation exercise, Sheriff aimed to help the partners discover which guests were in a position to give them new business and which were only there for the hospitality.

> "It was like a very sophisticated guessing game. I would keep a partner talking for half an hour and at the end of the exercise I would announce, guess what, I was a waste of time. I was not in a position to give you any business while the individual over there, who you ignored for most of the event, was looking to discuss a large project with you."

The full program of sessions covered skills like reviewing individuals' performance, putting together tenders, and negotiating skills. The most popular and best-attended were sessions on appraisal, team building, media skills, interviewing, and professional selling.

"I had to speed up the tutors," Sherrif explains.

> "Quantify, qualify, explain your statement. Remember that lawyers are like sponges when it comes to soaking up information and that they are very fast at analyzing statistical information. For God's sake, do not put up a statistic unless you know exactly where you got it from."

KEY LEARNING POINTS

» Boardroom and senior executives' forums will fail to engage their members unless the key individuals that shape the strategy or determine the future of the business are present and actively engaged in the discussions (ITT L&E and BPX).

» A neutral atmosphere of learning, away from day-to-day imperatives, will help to expose and resolve disagreements, rigid conformities, and unspoken but healthy consent between individual boardroom members or between the board and the senior management team (ITT L&E).

» The chair or chief executive must take the lead in championing the initiative and in briefing external contributors so that new concepts and good practice can be framed in the context of the business's current concerns (ITT L&E and RUC).

» External contributors should have direct experience of the sector or industry in which the business operates, or at the very least be able to demonstrate understanding of its front-line culture and concerns (RUC and Beachcroft Stanley).

Key Concepts and Thinkers

- » Why directors learn
- » What directors learn
- » When, where, and with whom
- » How directors learn (or don't).

The research and concepts that have helped shape boardroom education fall rather neatly into why, what, when, where, and how.

WHY DIRECTORS LEARN

The godfather of thought about why directors need further personal or management development after their appointment to the board is not one of the heavyweight US academics but an independent strategy consultant based in London and Hong Kong, **Bob Garratt**.

When Garratt first raised the question of director development in his 1988 book *The Learning Organization*, he was a voice in the wilderness. Now corporate collapses and scandals are so common that it seems that Garratt's basic premise – directors are promoted to the level of their inability, not ability, and the gaps in their capability only become evident when they screw up – must have been self-evident for decades. In fact it has only been a matter of years since this rather obvious statement of fact has been taken seriously.

In his early work, which arose out of his interest in organizational learning at all levels, Garratt fingered a lack of general management education as the principal constraint on a newly appointed director's ability to think strategically rather than manage tactically. Since no time or money is usually made available for directors to develop into their direction-giving role, they gradually slide back into the perspective and limited good practice of their old specialist role. At best, this results in them being excluded from the inner decision-making circles of the board. At worst, they actually get to make or influence decisions based on this narrow view of the world.

Later work by Garratt adapted the double-loop learning model of Harvard's Chris Argyris (see below), showing how individuals' ability to monitor and evaluate environmental changes from a broader strategic perspective enabled them to spot and respond to unexpected disruptions early enough to make a difference; and how a holistic attitude to performance and control systems helps them respond creatively to deviations from strategic plans lower down the organization.

He has also compiled a list of duties and attributes that should form the basis for any assessment of directors' performance and any educational initiative designed to improve it. These include:

» ensuring legitimacy (staying within the law);
» upholding their primary obligation (to the company not the shareholders);
» upholding their primary role (to drive the enterprise forward whilst keeping it under prudent control);
» holding the company in trust (for future generations);
» ensuring critical review and debate (around the boardroom table);
» upholding a duty of care (in risk assessment and decision taking);
» upholding the three values of effective corporate governance (accountability, probity, and transparency);
» upholding the rights of minority owners;
» ensuring corporate social responsibility; and
» ensuring the board learns, develops, and communicates.

For these duties to be respected, lived, and monitored, Garratt argues, it is essential that a director is inducted, included, and brought to directorial competence. This is the responsibility of the chair, not the chief executive. Directors must be respected for their individual inputs and encouraged to exercise their personal judgment. The law holds them both jointly and individually liable for their decisions and actions – although most directors do not understand this. Neither do they appreciate that they are.

Garratt was one of the first people to highlight the need for "learning leaders" and "learning boards" and the role of the chair in ensuring these concepts are sustained. Others have developed equally valuable work on how this can be achieved and these are covered later in this chapter. But he was the one who spotted that without this realization, corporate scandals of the type that has now engulfed corporate America were an inevitable result of a flawed system, rather than an aberration brought on by a few "bad apples."

WHAT DIRECTORS LEARN

As discussed in the chapter "What is Boardroom Education?", both research and in-company or business school programs center on three priorities.

The first is achieving the right structure and balance of responsibilities in line with modern thinking about *effective corporate governance*.

This covers issues such as the appointment and proper induction of non-executive directors, the training of newly appointed executive directors, and the formal development needed to create an effective balance of roles between the board chair and the company chief executive.

The conceptual framework for this task was laid down by two leading figures in the corporate governance debate in the early 1990s. In the United Kingdom a leading family member of the branded foods and drinks giant Cadbury-Schweppes, **Sir Adrian Cadbury**, was charged by the UK government to head up a committee to investigate urgent reforms to corporate board structure.

The resulting code of practice recommended that:

» Boards of directors, including three non-executives, must meet regularly and provide an effective lead and control of the business. The chair and chief executive should be separate roles.
» Non-executive directors (NEDs) should be independent, appointed for limited terms, and selected through a formal process by the whole board.
» Executive directors' contracts should not run for more than three years. Their pay, pension, and stock options should be monitored by a remuneration committee composed mainly of NEDs.
» The board, monitored by an audit committee of at least three NEDs, must give a clear, balanced assessment of the company's position, establishing that it is a going concern and confirming the efficacy of internal controls.

Figgy pudding

At the time, there were many expert commentators that observed that, without regulation or legislation to back up these proposals, they would prove little more than a fig leaf. Principal among these was Harvard Business School's Professor **Jay Lorsch**. In his 1989 book *Pawns or Potentates: The Reality of America's Corporate Boards*, Lorsch argued that the forces enhancing directors' powers – such as their sense of group solidarity and (where it existed) the open management style of the CEO – were outweighed by the numerous constraints on their ability to exercise it.

These included:

» the limited time, knowledge, and expertise of NEDs;
» a lack of consensus on essential corporate goals;
» group norms and protocols against:
  – criticizing the CEO
  – outside contact
  – discussing accountability; and
» the power of the CEO in terms of:
  – knowledge and expertise
  – control of the agenda
  – control of meetings
  – control of information
  – selection of directors.

Lorsch's conclusions, based on a survey of over 2000 directors in 1988, were that outside directors were incapable of standing up to the CEO in anything other than a serious crisis – by which time the damage to the corporation of their reticence will have already been done.

> "These talented, successful individuals meet infrequently and relatively briefly at tightly structured meetings with a full agenda. Busy themselves, they don't object to the boardroom norm discouraging extra-meeting contact. Add the norms that discourage open criticism of the CEO, and it's abundantly clear why directors find it hard to communicate freely with each other."

The all-embracing power of the CEO means that, unless the board is uncommonly united, individual directors will be unable to exercise much influence over corporate affairs. "Although directors feel they receive adequate information, their time, knowledge and interpretive ability are no match for those of a full-time and long-service CEO" Lorsch concludes. "Since the CEO determines what information directors receive, it is no exaggeration to say that, in most instances, directors understand the company through the CEO's eyes."

Pushing out the boundaries

The new stream of US corporate auditing scandals triggered by Enron and Worldcom have shown just how right Lorsch was. However, the first corporate governance scares in the early 1990s generated a welcome stream of new training initiatives that attempted to pick off and deal with the worst shortcomings he highlighted.

Specialist institutes like the Business Round Table and Corporate Board in the United States and the Institute of Directors in the United Kingdom have launched a series of courses, seminars, and workshops targeted at NEDs and newly appointed directors and covering the essential legal and fiduciary responsibilities they will have to grapple with (see the chapter "Resources").

A variety of new research and teaching centers have been set up in leading international business schools and independent management institutes. These have not only produced courses and programs on basic boardroom skills but pioneered consultancy-based training in the second major focus of modern boardroom education – *teamworking*, the second priority.

Principal among these has been the research and teaching center at the Cranfield School of Management, headed by Professor **Andrew Kakabadse**. His long-term research into international executive competencies (see the chapter "The Global Dimension") highlighted that the chief failing of boards was a failure to reach consensus on key corporate objectives and to put hard issues on the table.

Good teamwork was found to be critical. Directors' ability to work together to achieve a common vision of the future underpinned the best boards in a comprehensive survey that spanned 5000 managers in North America, Europe, and Asia.

"Respect for each other and maturity are essential," Kakabadse says.

"Executives on the board need to recognize that contributions from people who think and feel differently from themselves are equally valuable in a strategic debate. This becomes even more important in multinational companies, where an openness to other cultures and attitudes is a prerequisite to commercial success."

Specific personal qualities held by directors with the best track record – the inculcation of which still forms the basis of Cranfield's senior executive coaching today – include:

» having tact and sensitivity in managing people and teams;
» clearly communicating the objectives of the organization;
» making themselves available to receive feedback; and
» behaving in ways that support the policies and objectives they wish others to adopt.

In terms of this final "competency," for example, Kakabadse developed a diagnostic tool that enabled chief executives or chairs to measure how the individual decisions and behavior exhibited by key members of the board underpinned or undermined the collective values and points of principle of the whole.

Senior teambuilding: oxymoron in the making?

Lest the quest for the perfect senior team should otherwise dominate boardroom education, expert HR practitioners should read the conclusions of a study conducted in 1997 by a senior partner at McKinsey, **Jon Katzenberg**. His write-up of the findings in the November edition of *Harvard Business Review* sought to explode a few common myths about top-level teambuilding. The three most important were:

» *Teamwork at the top will lead to team performance.* Teamwork, in Katzenberg's view, is not the same as team performance. Teamwork is broad-based cooperation and supportive behavior; a team is a tightly focused performance unit. By concentrating all its attention on teamwork, the senior group is actually less likely to be discriminating about when and where it needs to apply the discipline to achieve real team performance. Members of senior groups may improve their ability to communicate and support one another, but they will not obtain team performance without applying team discipline.
» *Teams at the top need to spend more time together building consensus.* The truth, according to Katzenberg, is that most senior executives or main board directors have little time to spare, and the idea of spending more time struggling to build consensus often makes no sense to them. Many decisions, he argues, are better made individually. In any case, consensus may not be desirable. Real teams

do not avoid conflict – they thrive on it. And conflict is virtually unavoidable at the top.

» *The senior group should function together as a team whenever it is together.* Katzenberg argues that most senior leadership interactions are not team opportunities. A team is usually focused around a single or a few key purposes. Boardroom activities cover a diverse range of tasks. Team-based activity is usually most needed during negotiations for mergers and acquisitions or strategic alliances where critical issues cannot be resolved without integrating the skill sets of both organizations and where overlapping formal structures and processes require new informal networks.

Whether boards work as teams or not, all researchers in this field are united in thinking that what distinguishes effective boards is that they are robust, effective social systems. The most recent addition, **Jeffrey Sonnenfeld**, who founded Yale School of Management's Chief Executive Leadership Institute, argues that the meltdowns of companies like Enron, Wordcom, and Tyco occur less because of outright corruption or incompetence but because the chief executives failed to create a climate of trust and candor where legitimate and open dissent can take place and individuals do not get trapped in rigid, typecast positions.

Sonnenfeld's recommendations put conceptual flesh around the good practice of chairmen like SmithKlineBeecham's Henry Wendt in the early 1990s (see "The Global Dimension"). Directors should be given tasks that require them to inform the rest of the board about the strategic and operational issues the company faces. This may involve collecting external data, meeting customers, anonymously visiting plants and stores in the field, and cultivating links to outside parties critical to the company.

Similarly the chair should examine and monitor directors' confidence in the integrity of the enterprise, the quality of the discussions at board meetings, the credibility of reports, the use of constructive professional conflict, the level of interpersonal cohesion, and the degree of knowledge. In evaluating individual board members, the chair should also go beyond reputations, resumés, and skills and look at initiatives, roles, participation in discussions, and energy levels.

Henry V, humanism and horse whispering

The third focus for boardroom education is exposing directors to new practices, approaches, and ideas that their industry or company-based activities would not otherwise place before them.

In recent years, the emphasis has switched from benchmarking exercises or lectures by business gurus on new business practices or philosophies to examining the links between concepts and good practice in non-business fields.

The topics or activities can vary from ideas that are analogous or transferable to business to the totally unrelated and downright whacky.

» In Japan, senior managers at the cosmetic company Shiseido attend seminars to broaden their perspective, where speakers discuss topics as diverse as gymnastics and Japan's volunteer medical service in Zaire. A similar initiative at Kikkoman, Japan's largest maker of soy sauce, has senior managers being regularly chased out of the office to go "people watching" in Tokyo's liveliest shopping and entertainment areas. Middle managers attend breakfast meetings with the company president to make suggestions. "The experience is really stimulating," says managing director **Kenzaburo Mogu**. "Everyone is excited about bringing their ideas to the president."

» In the United States, Harvard's Professor **John Kotter** runs boardroom briefings that link the strategies of leading US military commanders such as George Washington, Sam Grant, and Dwight D. Eisenhower to business management. One of the more important conclusions is to equate wartime leadership with the management of change. To repeat John Kotter's quotation: "A peacetime army can usually survive with good administration up and down the hierarchy, coupled with good leadership at the very top. A wartime army, however, needs competent leadership at all levels. No one has figured out how to manage people effectively into battle – they must be *led*."

» In the United Kingdom, Cranfield School of Management has linked up with the Globe Theatre to launch the Praxis Centre, which offers a series of programs that discuss current management issues in the context of Shakespeare's plays. The sessions are led by **Richard Olivier**, son of the great Lord Olivier. Participants watch a play at the

Globe and then discuss the themes that emerge. "Stepping into Leadership with Henry V," for example, discusses how leaders step into the role, prove themselves to be worthy, and unite a disparate group around a common goal. "Exploring Leadership through the Merchant of Venice" looks at the special challenges that arise from managing a culturally diverse group such as whether feminine wisdom needs to disguise itself as male in order to be heard. In a separate and truly whacky initiative, the Manchester Business School has recently taken participants on its executive programs to stables to learn the art of "horse whispering" in an attempt to make them more sensitive communicators at work.

» In Italy, leading consultant **Alfredo Ambrosetti** runs the Alpha Plus, a learning "club" for chief executives and board directors who pay an annual subscription to attend monthly meetings facilitated by leading thinkers, politicians, philosophers, and journalists. Similarly in France, Professor **Henri-Claude de Bettignes** oversees the AVIRA program where 15 senior executives personally selected by de Bettignes meet to debate matters of mutual concern in Singapore, California, or on Insead's Fontainebleau campus. At a recent meeting a key topic was: "Can CEOs run companies according to humanist principles?" While this can prove a valuable way of helping directors "get outside" a problem so that they can see it more effectively, there is a danger in taking this process too literally.

The whole point of getting inspiration from a non-business discipline – be it history, philosophy, or anthropology – is that it can provide a useful framework for thinking about old problems in new ways. It works less well if it becomes an orthodoxy used to justify day-to-day actions or "prove" business philosophies that are wholly out of context with the original purpose of the work.

For instance, the chairman of Sony, **Norio Ohga**, a leading sponsor of classical music in Japan, recently compared running a business to conducting an orchestra. The principal conductor of the Chicago Philharmonic Orchestra, **Benjamin Zander**, profiting from the surge of interest this generated, has recently done the rounds of the business schools and international conferences with a cabaret-style presentation promoting the idea.

As an academic concept, the idea is very attractive. The analogy of a group of specialists, whose talents are brought together by a conductor with the complete score of the music, fits in well with the current emphasis on project leadership and creative teambuilding. However, the reality is that most conductors – as Zander himself admits – are unmitigated tyrants who only succeed in exacting the creative excellence they aspire to by bullying and sometimes abusing the musicians who work under them. If you really adopted their leadership style, half your subordinates would walk out on you overnight.

Similarly Oxford's top biologist, **Richard Dawkins**, whose bestselling book the *Selfish Gene* shattered the popular belief that evolution necessarily favors altruism and self-sacrifice, recently gave an interview to the *Harvard Business Review* in which he sounded a cautionary note about business gurus and consultants borrowing from all fields of science to theorize about organizational behavior and business strategy.

He points out, for example, that hardly any of the research on alpha males, which has been used in some management circles to explain why women are unsuited for business leadership, is relevant to humans. Evolutionary ideas should not be picked up in a simple way and care must be taken to distinguish between science and opinion. "It would be very dangerous for lay people to think that a scientist's opinion on such matters counts for anything," he concludes. "The job of a scientist is not to say 'I am a scientist and I believe such and such', but rather to say 'I'm a scientist, and let me explain what you need to do in order to decide for yourself'."

WHEN, WHERE, AND WITH WHOM

Our own research on this subject, conducted for Roffey Park, forms the basis of the earlier chapter "State of the Art." However, the essential points are.

» Senior managers and boardroom directors are most informed and inspired in their work by private research or feedback from their own networks.
» Informal networks are generally preferred to those created by boardroom forums, business school programs, or specialist consultancies.

» This is because executives and directors want control or influence over the topics they discuss and the people they discuss it with – finding the right "peer group" is critical in their eyes if they are to share ideas and experiences openly.

» Most feel better able to share and learn from new insight and concepts away from the immediate surroundings of their own offices or the company headquarters.

» Time is a critical factor: executives and directors want to control when as well as where they learn.

HR practitioners wanting to launch a new education initiative targeted at the board therefore face a considerable challenge. The way forward, discussed in "State of the Art" in more detail, is to design programs that give participants the freedom to choose or influence the peer group they study with, the topics they focus on, and the experts or speakers who will lead the sessions.

HOW DIRECTORS LEARN (OR DON'T)

By far the most interesting work on this subject is that of London Business School's **Charles Hampden Turner** in his book *Charting the Corporate Mind*. Hampden Turner uses the classic metaphor of the senior manager as a helmsman on a ship. From the helmsman's viewpoint he is engaged in a process of

» *leading* so that he can *learn* and *learning* so he can *lead*.
  His ship keeps
» *erring* so that it must be *corrected*.
  Steering this ship involves
» *maintaining* continuity in the midst of *change*.
  In holding to his course he is both
» the *cause* of the ship's position, yet affected by it.
  Each element in the system – wind, rudder, etc. – is
» *independent* of the other, yet *dependent* on it.
  All elements in the system can be
» analyzed as *parts*, yet they combine as a *whole.*

Hampden Turner uses the analogy because the endless dynamic of each gust of wind or the pull of the tide requiring a different response from the helmsman creates a "cybernetic loop" from which the modern field of cybernetics is inspired.

Continuous boardroom learning is essential in his view because without it the cybernetic loop turns vicious rather than virtuous. Just as newly appointed directors tend to fall back on their specialist roots if they feel disempowered by their new responsibilities, in Bob Garratt's model of boardroom learning (see above), so executives "at the helm" stick to a course that has been rendered invalid by changing circumstances as an inadvertent response to stress brought about by internal or external corporate conflict.

The anthropologist Gregory Bateson, to whom Hampden Turner turned as a source of inspiration, calls the process *schismogenesis*, "a growing split in the structure of ideas." Just as the helmsman keeps noting errors (in the course) and correcting them, so dilemmas do not go away but perpetually re-present themselves in changing forms and varieties.

Employees may develop (or regress) in their level of skills. Shareholders may prefer the bid of a corporate raider. Customers may change their tastes or grow more sophisticated. The environment may suddenly deteriorate, the community clamor, the government interfere. "Whether or not the executives have personally contributed to the split, they may be pulled apart by it psychologically," Hampden Turner stresses. "Because [resolving the] dilemma is so painful, many managers prefer to rend the system rather than rend themselves, yet this will blind the managers to the polarity they have rejected and may fatally cripple the organization's ability to learn."

The internal forces that drive decision makers down this destructive path were explored in more depth in a research project set up in 1996 by a team of academics from different departments of Harvard University who examined the neurobiological sources of defensive and non-rational behavior. The two professors representing the business school, finance expert **Michael Jensen** and a leading guru on organizational learning, **Chris Argyris**, are using the results to determine why chief executives persist in making decisions that are bound to damage their companies.

They have already concluded that the unconscious mechanisms which generate a "fight or flight" response in animals threatened by predators generate emotionally defensive behavior in humans. Equally important is that the signal generating fear in humans reaches the amygdala (the part of the brain at the back of the head which is responsible for our primal emotions) before it reaches the cortex (the front of the head responsible for rational thought). As a result, humans are driven into defensive and non-rational behavior by their natural instincts before they are able to temper these with logic or reflection.

The psychological forces that are unleashed if these natural instincts are not tempered is explored in more detail by London Business School's Manfred Kets de Vries in a 1989 report for the American Management Association on why leaders self-destruct. De Vries cites three forces that are particularly destructive and which are often revealed during professional counseling.

» Succession to top leadership positions in an organization is necessarily isolating in that it separates leaders from others (who now directly report to them) and leaves them without peers. As a result, their own normal dependency needs for contact, support, and reassurance rise up and overwhelm them.
» Whether consciously or unconsciously, employees expect their organization's leaders to be infallible and even gifted to some degree with "magical" powers.
» Troubled by guilt feelings about their success and fearful that it may not last, leaders may unconsciously cause themselves to fail.

"I am not suggesting that each business leader will resort to pathological behaviour on reaching the top," de Vries concludes. "What differentiates those that 'crash' from those that don't is the latter's ability to stay in touch with reality and take psychological forces in their stride."

KEY LEARNING POINTS

» Directors, if they have not received a general management education, will fall back on the narrow perspective of their specialist experience, to the detriment of the board, unless they are actively drawn into strategic discussions by the chair or chief executive.

» Non-executive directors will be unable to contribute effectively unless they are actively encouraged to visit and consult with both the sites of the business and its front-line managers, and the organization's key stakeholders. Negotiating access and designing a systematic program that will facilitate this is the responsibility of the chair, not the chief executive.

» Effective boards are underpinned by a robust social system. The rules and regulations regarding how many times the board meets, who attends, and what reporting systems are in place will yield nothing if, once assembled, individual members cannot balance open and frank discussion and dissent with the ability to reach a practical consensus. Systematic development may be needed to achieve this, particularly in the case of international boards with a non-homogeneous membership.

» Succession to the top position in any organization is a necessarily isolating experience. Chief executives will be unable to rely on internal peer support and their own normal dependency on contact and reassurance may rise up and overwhelm them unless a network of outside counterparts or external peers is put in place, either through their own efforts or through that of an HR specialist.

Resources

» Books
» Journals
» Courses and seminars
» E-learning providers
» List of addresses.

This chapter lists books, articles, and Websites that you may find useful in furthering your study of boardroom education. Some related publications are listed in Chapter 9 of the ExpressExec title *Management Development*.

BOOKS

On boardroom learning

Creating a Learning Organization: a Guide to Leadership, Learning and Development and *Fish Rot At the Head: the Crisis in Our Boardrooms,*by Bob Garratt, 1989

Bob Garratt is an independent consultant based in London and Hong Kong. His commitment to boardroom education was inspired by the research he undertook for his 1989 book on the learning organization, which suggested that the "Peter Principle" – executives are promoted to the limit of their *inability* – was alive and well in most boards.

The means by which directors can be developed to contribute effectively to their boards is discussed in more depth in the second book. Garratt has always seen boardroom learning and corporate governance hand in hand. For him, effective corporate governance is about the exercise of the complex relationships between ownership, power, trust, and anti-corruption processes in the boardroom. To be effective it must be as much concerned with generating wealth for society (board performance) as simply staying rigidly within the rules (board conformance). Board conformance is necessary but not sufficient. Sufficiency comes through the exercise of appropriate values, structures, and processes in a board to generate added value for the owners, private or public, to achieve their purpose within the laws of their country. Two models in the second book – covering the values directors should possess (accountability, probity, transparency) and a learning model based on their key functions (policy formulation/foresight, strategic management, supervisory management) – provide particularly good starting points for programmes assessing effective board behaviour.

Charting the Corporate Mind, by Charles Hampden Turner, Blackwell, Oxford, 1990

Excellent primer for anyone wanting a starting point on how to streamline and improve the thinking of senior executives, particularly in the context of coaching, mentoring, or counseling. Hampden Turner bases his understanding of the corporate mind on cybernetics, which derives its name from *kubernets*, the Greek word meaning "helmsman" or "steersman." Like the helmsman who stubbornly sticks to a pre-designated course even when the wind changes, chief executives fail because – possibly as a psychological reaction to extreme stress – they persist with a strategy that has been rendered redundant by a changed commercial climate. The approach is described in more detail in "Key Concepts and Thinkers."

On creativity and strategy determination

The Next Big Idea: Managing in the Digital Economy, by Carol Kennedy, Random House, New York, 2001

Very useful for anyone wanting to check out the upcoming concepts that the CEO and the board might like to get exposed to during a board-room education seminar. Kennedy is the leading authority on the work of the world's leading business gurus – she is also author of *Guide to Management Gurus*, published by Century in 1991 and now in its 4th fully updated edition. The book looks at the history of the "big" idea in business – covering Taylorism, total quality management, business process re-engineering, and emotional intelligence – and looks ahead to the broader social issues companies will have to confront as part of their greater global influence on people's lives. The chapter on how ideas are developed in organizations, which covers new concepts created by Toyota, General Electric, and Shell (among others), is partic-ularly good and might generate new thought on how it can be done by your own organization.

From .com to .profit: Inventing Business Models That Deliver Value and Profit, by Nick Earle and Peter Keen, Jossey-Bass, San Francisco, 2000

Business models are the stuff of boardroom thinking sessions and this book is particularly good at linking strategy to the "big" idea. The point of strategy is to help individuals choose between competing priorities. And, according to the authors, the big idea or dream, the company's ambition for the future, can promote a climate of values that helps people make choices for themselves – whether or not to commit to the organization. How people see the future of the organization, individually and collectively, will determine whether it achieves its goals. In this sense, as in politics, the "vision thing" is the key to strategy. Strategy today is nothing without the passion of the people implementing and building on it.

When Sparks Fly: Igniting Creativity in Groups, by Dorothy Leonard and Walter Swap. Harvard Business School Press, Boston, 1999

Although it is written for groups at any level in the organization, this book is as good as any in helping the designer of board-level brainstorms come up with new techniques and approaches. It emphasizes that group creativity depends more on managing the creative process as a whole than relying on a few "creatives." It includes plenty of exercises and ground rules that can be used to foster innovative thought, such as the role of "devil's advocates," role playing and scenarios, and provocative physical surroundings.

On corporate governance

New Directions in Corporate Governance, by Nick Kochan. Report No. 2137, Business International, London, 1991

Researched when the first outcry about corporate governance scandals was at its height (10 years before the Enron and Worldcom frenzy), this report was one of the first to suggest that beefing up the numbers of independent directors in an attempt to police boardroom ethics and decision making would prove useless if NEDs were not given the time, access, and inside information to keep abreast of what was going on. It also compares the contrasting way in which institutional investors exert their authority on either side of the Atlantic, with UK investors engaging in backroom lobbying and US counterparts laying down very public proxy votes at the AGM. Separate chapters cover the role and development of independent directors in Europe and Japan.

Pawns or Potentates: The Reality of America's Corporate Boards, by Jay Lorsch and Elizabeth MacIver, Harvard Business School Press, Boston, 1989

Lorsch's state-of-the-art assessment of the forces enhancing and undermining the power of directors could have been written yesterday rather than nearly 15 years ago. Long before the research of Yale's Jeffrey Sonnenfeld in 2001 suggested that the way people work together on boards, rather than rules and regulations, makes great boards great, Lorsch had his finger on the pulse. Apart from the obvious lack of time and knowledge hamstringing NEDs, Lorsch pointed to two killer factors. The first is the power of the chief executive in controlling the agenda and the flow of supporting data. The second is "group norms" that discourage criticism of the chief executive, contact with external stakeholders, and discussing accountability. The case for boardroom education has never been better made.

The Family Business: Its Governance for Sustainability, by Alden Lank and Fred Neubauer, Macmillan, London, 1989

It is not surprising that the best book on the governance structures of family firms was written by two academic experts at IMD, a top business school based in Switzerland. Family dynasties have spanned up to six generations in mainland Europe. They have done so by rigorous succession planning and development from an early age (see "The Global Dimension") and, as this book highlights, by creating the right institutional structures to manage the relationship between the family itself, the board of directors, and the executives in charge of running the company. Much of the educational work undertaken by IMD in its popular program "Leading the Family Business" is based on groups of executives and family owners tackling the practical issues involved in a sustained dialog. The approach and examples are set out in a number of chapters and provide a useful model for HR practitioners attempting the same goal.

See also *The Learning Organisation* and *Fish Rot at the Head*, by Bob Garratt, above.

On counseling and coaching

The Coaching Manager: Developing Top Talent in Business, by James Hunt and Joseph Weintraub, Sage Publications, London and California, 2002

Hot off the press at the time of the present title going to print is this detailed guide by two expert academics at Babson College in the United States. The book starts by distinguishing between mentoring and coaching and setting the basic principles of coaching in the context of Daniel Goleman's theories of emotional intelligence (see "State of the Art"). The model advocated by the authors covers elements such as creating the right environment, assessing who is and isn't "coachable," focusing on what is important, observing without inferring, providing balanced feedback, and setting goals. Hunt and Weintraub cover each of these in turn, using anonymized examples drawn from their own experience. They then pioneer the concept of "the coaching manager," looking at how this key role can be used at all levels of the organization. The authors do not focus particularly on board-level coaching, but many of the examples and the methods advocated are directly applicable.

Others

» *Great Leaders*, by John Adair, Talbot Adair Press, 1989.
» *Blown to bits. How the new economics of information transforms strategy*, by Philip Evans and Thomas S. Wurster, Harvard Business School Press, Boston, 1999.

JOURNALS

Harvard Business Review

In recent years, this noteworthy journal has focused its attention on issues relating to corporate governance, boardroom education, executive coaching, and senior management teams. The best articles include:

» Kotter, J.P. (1990) "What leaders really do," May–June.
» Taylor, B, Chait, R.P., and Holland, T.P. (1996) "The new work of the nonprofit board," September–October. (Introduction: "Is your board adding value or simply wasting its members' time?")

» Katzenbach, J. (1997) "The myth of the top management team," November–December. (Introduction: "Even in the best companies, a so-called top team seldom functions as a real team.")

» Drucker, P. (1999) "Managing oneself," March–April. (Introduction: "Success in the knowledge economy comes to those who know themselves – their strengths, their values, and how best they perform.")

» McFarlan, F. Warren (1999) "Working on non-profit boards: don't assume the shoe fits," November–December. (Introduction: "Most businesspeople will serve on the board of a nonprofit organization at some point. But the governance of nonprofits can differ dramatically from the governance of businesses.")

» Goleman, D. (2000) "Leadership that gets results," March–April. (Introduction: "New research suggests that the most effective executives use a collection of distinct leadership styles – each in the right measure, just at the right time. Such flexibility is tough to put into action, but it pays off in performance. And better yet, it can be learned.")

» Dawkins, R. (2001) "What is science good for?" January. (Introduction: "It's more popular than ever for business executives and management thinkers to use science to explain organizational dynamics, citing everything from complexity theory to the 'alpha male' in the boardroom. Has the borrowing gone too far?")

» Berglas, S. (2002) "Dangers of executive coaching," June. (Introduction: "In some companies, having a coach is a badge of honor. But many top managers are finding that the advisers hired to solve their performance only make matters worse.")

» Sonnenfeld, J. (2002) "What makes great boards great?," September. (Introduction: "It's not rules and regulations. It's the way people work together.")

Other articles

» Sinetar. M. (1985) "Entrepreneurs, chaos and creativity: can creative people survive large company structure," *Sloan Management Review*, Winter.

» Syrett, M. (1987) "Flying high with the chosen few," *Sunday Times*, August 16.

» Garratt, B. (1988) "Creating the culture for the learning organization: the challenge for learning leaders," Original paper published in *Frontiers of Leadership*, Blackwell, Oxford.

» Kets de Vries, M.F.R. (1989) "Leaders who self-destruct: the causes and cures," *Organisational Dynamics*, Spring. (Introduction: "Why do some people derail when they reach the top? Their ability to stay in touch with reality and take psychological pressures in their stride.")

» Dobrzynski, J. (1990) "A shareholder's place is in the boardroom – sometimes," *Business Week*, January 22.

» Belbin, M. (1992) "Solo leader/team leader: antithesis in style and structure," *Frontiers of Leadership*, Blackwell, Oxford.

» "On Trust: Increasing the effectiveness of charity trustees and management committees," Report of a working party on trustees set up by the NCVO and the Charity Commission, NCVO, 1992.

» Syrett, M. (1993) "Finding a place at the top table," *Daily Telegraph*, 26 August. (Introduction: "The Cadbury report has boosted demand for non-executive directors.")

» Kakabadse, A. (1995) "Common competencies," *Asia Pacific HR Monitor*, Economist Intelligence Unit (Asia), Quarter 4.

» Morris, R. (1995) "Cracking the Cadbury Code," *Management Today*, April. (Introduction: "The Cadbury Code of Practice on corporate governance has been described as ineffective and irrelevant. So will Cadbury Two be any different, or is statutory control now inevitable?")

» Neubauer, F. and Parikh, J. (1997) "Tales from the boardroom: the inside story," *MBA Magazine*, December.

» Neubauer, F. (1998) "Evaluating the performance of the board," *Forum* (journal of the European Forum for Management Development), **1**.

» Syrett, M. and Lammiman, J. (1998) "Innovation at the top: where directors get their ideas from," Roffey Park Institute

» Syrett, M. and Lammiman, J. (1999) "The top-up principle," *People Management*, 11 March. (Introduction: "What are the incentives for people to keep on learning and developing once they have reached the boardroom? Research suggests drawing on personal interests is the best way to motivate directors to widen their perspectives.")

» Vicere, A. (2000) "Ten observations on e-learning and leadership development," *Human Resource Planning*, November.
» Mather, P.M., Munro, M.C., and Sturmer, F. (2001) "Dot-com boards: not for the faint of heart." *Ivey Business Journal*, March.

COURSES AND SEMINARS

The combination of basic boardroom skills and a lateral cognitive approach to strategy is reflected in the content and approach of the programs for directors offered by the major international schools of professional institutes. Specialist institutes like the Conference Board in the United States or the Institute of Directors in the United Kingdom tend to provide courses on the basic skills of being a director, covering issues like finance for non-financial directors, the role of the company director, or the role of the non-executive director. The Institute of Directors also jointly runs a program "Good Practice: Key Decisions for Board Directors" with Henley Management College, based on Henley's recent research into the skills needed by boardroom directors and the IOD booklet "Good Practice for Directors – Standards for the Board." This workshop covers issues such as defining the roles and responsibilities of the board, assessing accountability to shareholders and other stakeholders, measuring and monitoring management's performance, and clarifying the role of the chair.

Henley's Centre for Boardroom Effectiveness, launched and directed by Professor Keith MacMillan, also provides a portfolio of courses and seminars of its own, supported by original research, including an annual convention on corporate governance and boardroom education, held every autumn.

Other programs tackle the more complex issues of behavior and perception. At IMD in Lausanne, an international program for board members is based on course director Professor Neubauer's recent research into the effectiveness of boards, which created a series of diagnostic tools on how well the board is structured and the role of key individuals. The heart of the three-day workshop is an exchange of ideas based on contributions by the board chairs of prestigious European companies such as Cadbury-Schweppes or Siemens. The discussions cover the composition and working style of boards, the role of the CEO and top management, the influence and role of shareholders and other stakeholders, and the role of auditors.

A contrast in approach is provided by the London Business School's Directors' Forum. Developed in conjunction with Wharton Business School in the United States and the management consultancy KPMG, this original course takes the form of a two-day role playing exercise. Recently appointed directors grapple with the problems of running a major public company, using a fictitious organization MegaMicro, which has sales of over £1.2 billion and four divisions. New technology and competitors are now making inroads into the company's market share, turnover among senior managers is on the up, and margins are eroding. Using Wharton's "living case" teaching methods, participants examine issues such as board liability, succession, product liability, and the role of institutional investors.

For more senior directors, there are a number of programs which assemble CEOs or main board directors from international companies and industries and expose them to ideas or concepts that rarely feature in their day-to-day work. Good examples are the Insead program AVIRA, where 15 top executives, personally selected by the program's Professor Henri-Claude de Bettignes, meet to debate matters of mutual concern in Singapore, California, or on Insead's Fontainebleau campus; and the Alpha-Plus program run by the Italian management guru Alfredo Ambrosetti, where CEOs and boardroom directors pay an annual subscription to attend monthly meetings presided over by world-class thinkers, politicians, philosophers, and journalists.

E-LEARNING PROVIDERS

» AthenaOnline (US Institute for Management Studies http://www.thenewleader.com): "AthenaOnline is a premier publisher of multimedia training, education and career development products. We are an Internet 'knowledge network' headquartered in the San Francisco Bay Area, California."
» Caliber Learning Network (http://www.caliberlearning.com): "Calibre is the world's leading developer and distributor of Internet-based training and business communication solutions to corporations and institutions."

» Centra (http://www.centra.com): "Web-based software and services for live collaboration, enabling business interaction, collaborative commerce and corporate learning."

» click2learn.com (http://www.click2learn.com): "A leading provider of full service e-Learning solutions to businesses, government agencies and educational institutions throughout the world."

» Corporate University X-Change (http://www.corpu.com): "A corporate education research and consulting firm that assists organizations in optimizing their learning resources."

» DigitalThink (http://www.digitalthink.com): "DigitalThink is the leader in designing, developing and deploying e-learning solutions to Fortune 1000 companies."

» Docent (http://.www.docent.com): "Docent is a provider of eLearning products and services that enable the Web-based exchange of personalized and measurable knowledge within and among large enterprises, education content providers and professional communities."

» Eduventures.com (http://www.eduventures.com): "Eduventures. com Inc is a provider of education technology industry analysis, market data and insight to buyers, suppliers and users of e-learning products and services."

» Executive Development Associates (http://www.executivedevelopment.com): "Executive Development Associates (EDA) is a leading education and consulting firm specializing in the strategic use of executive/leadership development."

» Forum Corporation (http://www.forum.com): "A global leader in workplace learning ... pioneering new ways to achieve business results through learning. We specialize in creating innovative solutions that help companies build competitive advantage and lasting customer loyalty."

» FT Knowledge (http://.www.ftknowledge.com): "FT Knowledge is one of the world's leading providers of business education and management development. We specialize in providing learning and development that is highly relevant to the needs of business and those who work within it."

» Institute for Management Studies (http://www.ims-online.com): "A leader in executive education and management development for over

25 years, IMS holds one-day workshops on cutting edge management issues, taught by leading business school professors from the graduate schools at Harvard, University of Pennsylvania, UC Berkeley, Penn State, Stanford, SMU, Georgetown and others.''

» Knowledge Universe (KU) (http://www.knowledgeu.com): ''Knowledge Universe (KU) operates, incubates and invests in leading companies that build human capital by helping organizations and individuals to realise their full potential.''

» Parthenon Group (http://www.parthenon.com): ''The Parthenon Group ... provide[s] strategic advisory consulting services to business leaders who demand seasoned counsel and seek true business insights that yield results.''

» Pensare (http://www.pensare.com): ''Pensare develops Knowledge Community online learning solutions that drive teamwork, creativity and business results through the innovative use of strategic alliances, validated content, leading technology, applied learning tools, human interaction and cultural adaptation.''

» Provant (http://www.provant.com): ''We provide integrated solutions that resolve performance-based organizational challenges.''

» Quisic (http://www.quisic.com): ''Your freeline resource for the most current business thinking on the web. Business education solutions for corporations and academic institutions.''

» Saba (http://www.saba.com): ''Saba is a leading provider of e-learning infrastructure, which consists of Internet-based learning management systems, business to business learning exchanges and related services.''

» SmartForce (http://www.smartforce.com): ''Smartforce is redefining learning for the Internet age with its first of a kind, fully integrated, Internet-based e-Learning technology.''

» SMGnet-Strategic Management Group (http://www.smgnet.net/homei.htm): ''SMGnet, the online learning, development and Group delivery division of Strategic Management Group, Inc., concentrates on solving business issues by supporting the growth and development of human capital via the Internet.''

» Tacit (http://www.tacit.com): ''Tacit Knowledge Systems, Inc, is a pioneer and leader in providing automated knowledge discovery and exchange systems that, for the first time, offers organizations automated access to explicit, tacit and even private knowledge."

» The Learning Partnership (TLP) (http://www.tlp.org): "The Learning Partnership is owned by some of the world's leading business academies. Our mission is to create and share knowledge around the key issues facing business in the new Millennium."

» Unext (http://www.unext.com): "Unext was created to deliver world class education. We are building a scalable education business that delivers the power of knowledge around the world."

Source: Al Vicere, Smeal College of Business Administration, 2000.

LIST OF ADDRESSES

» American Assembly of Collegiate Schools of Business (AACSB)
600 Emerson Road, Suite 300
St Louis
MO 63141–6762
USA
Tel: +1 314 8728481
Fax: +1 314 8728495
Website: http://www.aacsb.edu

» The Anderson School at UCLA
110 Westwood Plaza
Box 951481
Los Angeles
CA 90095–1481
United States
Tel: +1 310 8256944
Fax: +1 310 8258582
Website: http://www.anderson.ucla.edu

» Arthur D Little School of Management
194 Beacon Street
Chesnut Hill
MA 012167
United States

Tel: +1 617 5522877
Fax: +1 617 5522051
E-mail: adlschool.mgmt@adlittle.com
Website: http://www.adlsom.com

» Ashridge Management College
Ashridge
Berkhamsted
Hertfordshire
HP4 1NS
United Kingdom
Tel: +44 1442 841000
Fax: +44 1442 841306
E-mail: info@ashridge.org.uk

» The Association of Business Schools
344/354 Gray's Inn Road
London
WC1X 8BP
United Kingdom
Tel: +44 171 837 1899
Fax: +44 171 837 8189
E-mail: 106262.227@compuserve.com
Website: http://www.leeds.ac.uk/bes/abs/abshome.htm

» Association for Management Education and Development
14–15 Belgrave Square
London
SW1X 8PS
United Kingdom
Tel: +44 171 235 3505
Fax: +44 171 235 3565
E-mail: amed.office@anet.demon.co.uk

» Association of Management Development Institutions in South Asia
8-2-333/A Road No 3 Banjara Hill
Ind–Hyderabad 500034
India
Tel: +91 40 244089
Fax: +91 40 244801

» Association of MBAs
  15 Duncan Terrace
  London
  N1 8BZ
  United Kingdom
  Tel: +44 171 837 3375
  Fax: +44 171 278 3634
» Berkeley – see Haas School of Business
» Bocconi – see SDA Bocconi
» Business Association of Latin American Studies
  c/o School of Business Administration
  University of San Diego
  5998 Alcala Park
  San Diego
  CA 92110
  United States
  Tel: +1 619 2604836
  Fax: +1 619 2604891
  E-mail: dimon@acusd.edu
» University of Cambridge – Judge Institute of Management Studies
  Trumpington Street
  Cambridge
  CB2 1AG
  United Kingdom
  Tel: +44 1223 337051/2/3
  Fax: +44 1223 339581
  Website: http://www.jims.cam.ac.uk/mba
» Central and East European Management Development Association
  Brdo pri Kranju
  4000 Kranj
  Slovenia
  Tel: +386 64 221–761
  Fax: +386 64 222–070
  E-mail: CEEMAN@IEDC-BRDO.SI
» Centre for High Performance Development
  Elvetham Hall

Hartley Wintney
Hampshire
RG27 8AS
United Kingdom
Tel: +44 1252 842677
Fax: +44 1252 842564
E-mail: info@chpd.co.uk

» China Europe International Business School
Jiatong University, Minhang Campus
800 Dong Chuan Road
Shanghai 200240,
Peoples' Republic of China
Tel: +8621 6463 0200
Fax: +8621 6435 8928

» The Chinese University of Hong Kong
Faculty of Business Administration
Leung Kau Kui Building
Shatin, New Territories
Hong Kong
PRC
Tel: +852 609 7642
Fax: +852 603 5762

» City University Business School
Frobisher Crescent
Barbican Centre
London
EC2Y 8HB
United Kingdom
E-mail: cubs-postgrad@city.ac.uk
Website: http//www.city.ac.uk/cubs

» Columbia Business School
Uris Hall
3022 Broadway
New York
NY 10027
United States
Tel: +1 212 8541961

Fax: +1 212 6662754
Website: http://www.columbia.edu
» Cranfield School of Management
Cranfield
Bedford
MK43 0AL
United Kingdom
Tel: +44 1234 751122
Fax: +44 1234 751806
Website: http://www.cranfield@ac.uk/som
» EM Lyon
23 avenue Guy de Collongue
BP 174
69132 Ecully Cédex
France
Tel: +33 4 78337865
Fax: +33 4 78336169
Website: http://www.em-lyon.com
» European Foundation for Management Development
88 rue Gachard
B-1050 Brussels
Belgium
Tel: +32 2 648 0385
Fax: +32 2 646 0768
E-mail: info@efmd.be
Website: http://www.efmd.be
» European Institute for Advanced Studies in Management
Rue d'Egmont 13
B-1000 Brussels
Belgium
Tel: +32 2 5119116
Fax: +32 2 5121929
» Graduate Management Admission Council (GMAC)
8300 Greensboro Drive
Suite 750
Mclean
VA 22102

United States
Tel: +1 703 7490131
Fax: +1 703 749169
E-mail: gmacmail@gmac.com
Website: http://www.gmat.org
» Haas School of Business
University of California at Berkeley
S440 Student Services Building
No 1902
Berkeley
CA 94720–1902
United States
Tel: +1 510 6421405
Fax: +1 510 6436659
Website: http://www.haas. berkeley.edu
» Harvard Business School
Soldiers Field
Boston
MA 02163
United States
Tel: +1 617 4956127
Fax: +1 617 4969272
Website: http://www.hbs.edu
» HEC School of Management
1 rue de la Liberation
78351 Jouy-en-Joas Cédex
France
Tel: +33 1 39677379/7382
Fax: +33 1 39677465
Website: http://www.hec.fr
» Henley Management College
Greenlands
Henley-on-Thames
Oxfordshire
RG9 3AU
United Kingdom
Tel: +44 1491 571454

Fax: +44 1491 571635
E-mail: info@henley.co.uk
Website: http://www.henleymc.ac.uk
» IESE – International Graduate School of Management
University of Navarra
Avenida Pearson 21
08034 Barcelona
Spain
Tel: +34 93 2534229
Fax: +34 93 2534343
Website: http://www.iese.edu
» IMD (International Institute for Management Development)
Chemin de Bellerive 23
PO Box 915
CH 1001 Lausanne
Switzerland
Tel: +44 41 21 618 0111
Fax: +44 41 21 618 0707
E-mail: info@imd.ch
Website: http://www.imd.ch
» Imperial College Management School
53 Prince's Gate
Exhibition Road
London
SW7 2PG
United Kingdom
Tel: +44 171 5949205
Fax: +44 171 8237685
E-mail: m.school@ic.ac.uk
Website: http://ms.ic.ac.uk
» INSEAD
Boulevard de Constance
77305 Fontainebleau Cédex
France
Tel: +33 1 60 72 40 00
Fax: +33 1 60 74 55 00
Website: http://www.insead.fr/

» Institute for Employment Studies
Mantell Building
University of Sussex
Brighton
BN1 9RF
United Kingdom
Tel: +44 1273 686751
Fax: +44 1273

» Institute of Personnel and Development
IPD House
Camp Road
London
SW19 4UX
Tel: +44 181 971 9000

» Leonard N Stern School of Business
New York University
44 West 4th Street
New York
NY 10012–1126
United States
Tel: +1 212 9980600
Fax: +1 212 9954231
Website: http://www.stern.nyu.edu

» London Business School
Sussex Place
Regents Park
London
NW1 4SA
United Kingdom
Tel: +44 171 262 5050
Fax: +44 171 724 7875
Website: http://www.lbs.ac.uk

» Lyon – see EM Lyon

» Manchester Business School
Booth Street West
Manchester
M15 6PB

United Kingdom
Tel: +44 161 2757139
Fax: +44 161 2756556
Website: http://www.mbs.ac.uk

» Massachusetts Institute of Technology – see MIT Sloan School of Management

» University of Michigan Business School
701 Tappan Street
Ann Arbor
MI 48109–1234
United States
Tel: +1 734 7635796
Fax: +1 734 7637804
Website: http://www.bus.umich.edu

» MIT Sloan School of Management
Massachusetts Institute of Technology
50 Memorial Drive
Cambridge
MA 02142
United States
Tel: +1 617 2533730
Fax: +1 617 2536405
Website: htp://web.mit.edu/sloan/www/

» The Open University Business School
Walton Hall
Milton Keynes
MK7 6AA
United Kingdom
Tel: +44 1908 653449
Fax: +44 1908 654320
Website: http://www.oubs.open.ac.uk

» Roffey Park Management Institute
Forest Road
Horsham
West Sussex
United Kingdom
Tel: +44 1293 851644

Fax: +44 1293 851565
E-mail: info@roffey-park.co.uk
» SDA Bocconi
Masters Division
Via Balilla 16–18
20136 Milan
Italy
Tel: +39 2 58363281
Fax: +39 2 58363275
Website: http://www.sda.uni-bocconi.it
» Stanford Graduate School of Business
Stanford University
Stanford
CA
United States
Tel: +1 650 7232766
Fax: +1 650 7257831
Website: http://gsb-www.stanford.edu
» Stern – see Leonard N Stern School of Business
» Strathclyde Graduate Business School
199 Cathedral Street
Glasgow
G4 0QU
United Kingdom
Tel: +44 141 5536118/9
Fax: +44 141 5528851
Website: http://www.strath.ac.uk/Department/SGBS
» Sundridge Park Management Centre
Plaistow Lane
Bromley
Kent
BR1 3TP
United Kingdom
Tel: +44 181 313 3131
» The Thinking Partnership
79, St John Street
London

EC1M 4NR
United Kingdom
Tel: +44 (0)20 7549 0440
E-mail info@thethinkingpartnership.com
Website: www.thethinkingpartnership.com
» UCLA – see The Anderson School at UCLA
» Warwick Business School
University of Warwick
Coventry
CV4 7AL
United Kingdom
Tel: +44 1203 523922
Fax: +44 1203 524643
Website: http://www.wbs.warwick.ac.uk
» Wharton School
University of Pennsylvania
102 Vance Hall
3733 Spruce Street
Philadelphia
PA 19104
United States
Tel: +1 215 8986183
Fax: +1 215 8980120
Website: http://www.wharton.upenn.edu

Ten Steps to Making it Work

1 Defining the need: group work, not teamwork
2 Defining the group: who's in, who's out
3 Time and location: short cuts or blind alleys
4 Getting the buy-in: miss it, miss out
5 Choosing the venue: where the five stars count
6 Briefing speakers: how to avoid loose cannons
7 Framing the initiative: converting off-the-shelf thinking
8 Sustaining the momentum: coping with the boredom threshold
9 Insider help: the chair or chief executive as champion
10 Section on personal coaching.

Designing and delivering an education initiative for the board involves actions very similar to those of any management development program. However the challenge is that much greater because, unlike participants nominated for other courses, the individuals you are dealing with can say "no."

1. DEFINING THE NEED: GROUP WORK, NOT TEAMWORK

In the chapter "Key Concepts and Thinkers," we highlighted the research of the McKinsey consultant Jon Katzenberg. This suggests that apart from when they participate in cross-company work during a merger or alliance, boardroom directors are not united by the kind of single purpose or outcome that bonds a functional team lower down in the organization.

The education needs of boards are complex and multifarious. Individuals will reach director status by different routes. Some get there because of their specialist or industry-specific track record; others, particularly non-executives, because they bring an outsider's perspective to key decisions. Some have benefitted from a comprehensive management education, including an MBA degree or participation in either an in-company or open executive program. Others have only their work experience to fall back on. Newly appointed executives may require basic training in the legal or fiduciary responsibilities of a director. Older directors may need more exposure to ideas and good practice outside the industry to combat a "business as usual" mentality.

HR practitioners responsible for boardroom education will therefore need to combine a series of individual initiatives designed to fill the gaps in the experience or knowledge of individuals with group work designed to provide a common starting point in discussions about strategy or key objectives.

2. DEFINING THE GROUP: WHO'S IN, WHO'S OUT

If the learning is collective, there is an immediate trade-off to consider: the bigger the group, the greater the difficulty in getting regular attendance and a solid sign-up. If the purpose of the exercise requires the attendance of, say, non-executives on the board, busy members of the senior management team, or outside stakeholders (e.g. senior managers from other companies in a strategic alliance, investors, or trade union representatives) then the task will be that much harder.

The decision about how many of the board are involved will ultimately depend on how inclusive or exclusive strategy determination is. There will always be the tendency to confine membership of new educational initiatives to the people who make the key decisions. Small numbers of directors who work and visit the company regularly are obviously easier to cater for than a large international group of independent directors and other external stakeholders.

Yet the revolution that gave birth to boardroom learning (see ''What Is Boardroom Education?'') was fueled by the realization that company strategy is often determined by a narrow elite of executives who are too homogeneous and close to the problems to frame their decisions in a broad enough context. The time pressures and incentives influencing the ability or willingness of directors to sign up may push both the sponsors and facilitators of boardroom learning initiatives to cut corners and limit membership; this goes against the grain of many of the desired goals.

Judicious use of the right location and timing (see below), e-mail, or video conferencing follows through and the commitment and active participation of the chairman and/or chief executive has, as this guide has shown, made it possible to engage a much wider group of people than might have been possible a decade ago. Anything is possible, if the key officers of the company are genuinely committed to the task.

3. TIME AND LOCATION: SHORT CUTS OR BLIND ALLEYS

Pragmatism and idealism are also contending opposites in this equation. Using the company boardroom or training premises, organizing the initiative around lunchtime sessions, or latching sessions onto the end of routine boardroom meetings may increase the likelihood of regular attendance, but ''fitting in'' the learning in this way is not conducive to long-term or blue-sky thinking.

A long weekend in a luxury hotel or stately home is not necessarily the only alternative. The Ambrosetti Consulting Group ran a highly successful boardroom program called Alpha Plus in which chief executives and directors from different companies hosted meetings in their own boardrooms for a half-day of intense discussion.

Putting psychological distance between participants and their day-to-day surroundings is the point of the exercise. The geographic location is only one factor in achieving this. A different space and time can be created.

4. GETTING THE BUY-IN: MISS IT, MISS OUT

One of the perquisites of seniority is the right to say no. Top managers are fussy about what they learn and who they learn with. They instinctively prefer expanding their existing knowledge and testing new ideas through their own personal networks with close professional colleagues they know and trust. The more formal the mechanism and the less control they have over the agenda and participants, the more distrustful they tend to become.

Apply peer pressure. If initially skeptical individuals become convinced that they are missing out because essential intellectual groundwork is being discussed in tandem with key company officers – who always attend and who feed back conclusions and insights during routine boardroom or strategy meetings – it is surprising how suddenly they are able to find the time to attend.

Let them influence and shape the agenda, picking up unexpected themes and issues from previous sessions and building them into new topics, complete with the appropriate outside experts or case examples. Capture the learning that emerges from the discussions and feed it back to the whole group and a wider audience. Give the impression in all these activities that what takes place in these sessions will influence the future of the organization. Then watch them queue up.

5. CHOOSING THE VENUE: WHERE THE FIVE STARS COUNT

Selecting a venue for board-level directors, particularly from blue-chip organizations, is a more rigorous task than choosing one for a less senior group. However grand the grounds and "listed" the building, and however well recommended the chef, a big-budget country house or up-market conference center will not necessarily provide you with the support or service you need.

Flexibility and common sense are often in short supply. Conference staff often trade on the classy looks of the rooms and assume that if they provide the basic off-the-shelf equipment and the standard pattern of meals and drinks receptions, they can leave you to your own devices and turn their attention to other matters. Getting them, for example, to lay on a buffet supper in the conference room at short notice rather than the sit-down meal you had originally ordered, or keep staff on and facilities open after hours so an expectedly fruitful session can be extended, is often too much to ask.

Where truly first-grade venues earn their stars is their ability and willingness to put themselves out on your behalf, rather than fitting you around their own pre-planned logistical requirements. This will not be evident from the glossiness of the brochure or the slickness of the conference manager's patter. Hard questioning is required to find out the limits of their resources and the training and experience of the staff who will actually come into contact with your top people. Severe loss of face back at the office is the price you will pay if you take everything on trust. Always visit, always ask to see the front-line staff, and preferably ask for (and follow up) references from previous users or organizations of a similar calibre.

6. BRIEFING SPEAKERS: HOW TO AVOID LOOSE CANNONS

What counts for venues counts for guest speakers. They also trade on good looks and reputation. Their willingness to be flexible usually extends only to the length of time you want them to speak and their ability to throw in a few sector-specific examples and anecdotes, rather than demonstrating a genuine commitment to tailor the conclusions of their latest Harvard-published book or pet theory to the specific learning issues of the group.

Make experts earn their exorbitant fee. Capture their interest by devising with them firm- or group-specific exercises or projects that will throw new light on their research or demonstrate new possibilities for their tools and techniques. Encourage them to feed back insights and conclusions sparked by these exercises in the wider context of their global work. Insist, wherever possible, that they do not parachute in and jet out of the session but take part in resulting discussions. Capture what emerges. Otherwise you might just as well save yourself the money and hire a video.

7. FRAMING THE INITIATIVE: CONVERTING OFF-THE-SHELF THINKING

However flexible the external contributors, the task of making the program relevant is down to you. Short pre-course assignments, scenario-based exercises developed specifically for the event, and syndicate and plenary discussions should all be used to take the concepts or good practice on show and ask, ''What does it mean for us?'' Capture what emerges and use it to inform discussions in future sessions, so that over time you build up a valuable store of firm-specific concepts and techniques that are inspired by new ideas outside the organization but shaped and reconfigured by the firm's own circumstances.

8. SUSTAINING THE MOMENTUM: COPING WITH THE BOREDOM THRESHOLD

Boredom thresholds and attention spans diminish with seniority. Keep them sustained by changing the format, approach, or location of each session. Feed back the conclusions of early sessions and encourage key company officers to build them into fully fledged strategic initiatives. Expand the scope and dimensions of the discussion over time so that it does not become mechanistic or samey. Encourage everyone to see the initiative: a think-tank that is laying down the intellectual groundwork for the organization's future.

9. INSIDER HELP: THE CHAIR OR CHIEF EXECUTIVE AS CHAMPION

Boardroom education is no different from any other organizational initiative. The inspiration may be sparked by someone else but unless the chair or chief executive work together championing and shaping it, nobody else will sign up.

Encourage the chair to see him- or herself as the guardian of the boardroom's education. Convince the chief executive that this kind of development activity is essential if strategy is to be informed and inspired by the latest thinking and good practice. Demonstrate to both officers that the board will work better for it. Ensure that they take a lead in all consultations that inform the design, approach, and good running of the initiative. Make sure that they attend regularly and are seen to take an active role, not only in formal presentations but also in the discussions and their evaluation.

10. SECTION ON PERSONAL COACHING

Insist that all newly appointed directors are given a formal induction outlining the essential activities of the organization and (if needed) spelling out the legal and fiduciary responsibilities that accompany the role. Regularly appraise their role, in collaboration with the board chair.

Bear in mind *always* that shortcomings in performance and inappropriate management styles often mask personality problems that may not be resolved by conventional boardroom coaching. Insist that every executive slated to receive coaching first receives a psychological evaluation. Screen out those that are not psychologically prepared or predisposed to benefit from the process. Hire independent mental health professionals to review coaching outcomes.

Frequently Asked Questions (FAQs)

Q1: What makes directors and board-level executives any different to develop than other managers?

A: They can say no. They cannot be forced to take part. They are picky about what they learn and who they learn with. They often work for other organizations. They bore easily and have the status to be able to show it. You get it in the neck rather than them if the initiative is a failure.

Q2: How do directors and board-level executives learn?

A: Through demonstrated good practice in other comparable organizations. Through the feedback of someone they trust and respect. Through reflection prompted by personal reading or private leisure or community-based activities. By making connections.

Q3: What role can the chief executive play?

A: Seeing the initiative as an essential part of strategy determination. Taking part regularly, not only in the formal proceedings but also in the design, syndicate discussions, and evaluation. Briefing external experts and contributors. Evaluating the conclusions in the wider context of the company's strategy and/or main aims. Taking part in feedback. Building suggestions, insights, and new concepts or techniques into "follow-through" initiatives.

Q4: What role can the chair play?

A: Taking the lead in setting up the initiative. Integrating it into a broader program of boardroom development and activity. Championing it as an essential prerequisite to good corporate governance. Involving and engaging key stakeholders (e.g. investors, regulators) in the process.

Q5: What role does the HR practitioner play?

A: Pointing out the need. Engaging the chair and chief executive. Defining the group. Overseeing or undertaking the design. Choosing the timing and location. Choosing and briefing the speakers. Overseeing or directly facilitating the syndicate and plenary discussions. Capturing the conclusions. Feeding back and building on the output. Ensuring that methods used, for example in coaching individuals, are appropriate to the circumstances and the participants.

Q6: What role do external consultants play?

A: Contributing methods, strategies, tools, and techniques or industry knowledge that are not available in-house. These should be assessed and integrated into the initiative by either a front-line executive or an HR practitioner with the expertise to assess their effectiveness and the in-company knowledge to set them in context. Often external consultants working with an HR practitioner who is acting in an internal consultancy capacity (and can therefore step back a pace and see the organization's needs in a broader perspective) is the best combination.

Q7: What role do coaches and counselors play?

A: Providing non-critical feedback and support to enable individual executives to assess and resolve personal issues that are affecting their performance. This often touches on deeply rooted personality problems that may not be easily resolved by conventional coaching. It is therefore very important that someone with the right expertise assesses whether the individual is "coachable" and whether the methods used by the provider are appropriate.

Q8: How can boardroom learning be sustained?

A: Through follow-up sessions and e-mail or intranet exchanges. Unfortunately this can be hampered, at board level, by the fact that some directors are still technology-shy and that an unwillingness to follow through can be easily masked behind a busy schedule that no subordinate can question.

Q9: How should initiatives be assessed?

A: By the quality of the output and their value to the organization. By the number of further initiatives they inspire. By the way they inform and inspire future strategic discussions. By the better interaction, cohesion, consultation, and inclusiveness they inspire in routine board behavior. By the transparency and trust – and thus good corporate governance – they bring to routine boardroom dealings. By the greater self-confidence they inspire in individuals.

Q10: Is this approach transferable?

A: Yes. It is applicable to anyone in a position of trust, including charitable trustees, school governors, directors of non-profit organizations, executives on health care trusts or police boards, partners in professional practices, and members of government quangos.

Index

EXPRESSEXEC –
BUSINESS THINKING AT YOUR FINGERTIPS

ExpressExec is a 12-module resource with 10 titles in each module. Combined they form a complete resource of current business practice. Each title enables the reader to quickly understand the key concepts and models driving management thinking today.

Available from:
www.expressexec.com

Customer Service Department
John Wiley & Sons Ltd
Southern Cross Trading Estate
1 Oldlands Way, Bognor Regis
West Sussex, PO22 9SA
Tel: +44(0)1243 843 294
Fax: +44(0)1243 843 303
Email: cs-books@wiley.co.uk

Printed and bound in the UK by
CPI Antony Rowe, Eastbourne

Printed and bound by CPI Group (UK) Ltd, Croydon, CR0 4YY

13/04/2025

14656561-0002